TURKISH
in a week

Tayfun Çağa and Gillian Çağa

Series Editors
Shirley Baldwin and Sarah Boas

Headway · Hodder & Stoughton

ACKNOWLEDGMENTS

The authors and publishers would like to thank the following for permission to reproduce copyright material:

Barnaby's Picture Library for the photo on page 57 (top); J Allan Cash for the photos on pages 25 (top), 42, 59; G Payne for the photos on pages 20, 33, 73 and 74; P and P F James for the photo on page 1; Feature-Pix for the photo on page 63; NASA/ Science Photo Library for the photo on page 54; Spectrum Colour Library for the cover photo; Richard Turpin for the photos on pages 7, 10, 15, 25 (bottom), 37 and 64.

All other photographs supplied by courtesy of Tayfun Çağa and S Üçtaşlı.

British Library Cataloguing in Publication Data

Caga, Tayfun
 Turkish in a week. – (In a week).
 1. Language. Turkish. Spoken
 I. Title II. Series
 494.3583421

 ISBN 0 340 50005 0

First published in Great Britain 1990

© 1990 Tayfun Çağa

Printed in Great Britain for the educational publishing division of Hodder and Stoughton Ltd, Mill Road, Dunton Green, Sevenoaks, Kent by Cambus Litho, East Kilbride.

CONTENTS

Introduction
Pronunciation guide

INTRODUCTION

Turkish is spoken by more than 150 million people from north-west China to the Balkans in about 26 different dialects. It is an easy language with a grammatical structure resembling that of Latin.

Modern Turkish is written in the Roman alphabet containing 21 consonants (excluding q, w and x) and 8 vowels which are classified as front (*soft*) vowels (**e**, **i**, **ö**, **ü**) and back (*hard*) vowels (**a**, **ı**, **o**, **u**).

Vowel Harmony Rule

The backbone of the language is the vowel harmony rule which dictates simply that if the vowel of the first syllable of a word is a front (or back) vowel, the vowels of subsequent syllables must also be front (or back) vowels. This means that the suffixes added to the words must be formed in accordance with the *sound* as well as with the person and tense of the verb or the function and number of the noun.

Pronunciation guide

1 There are no diphthongs and each letter retains its individual sound. A diphthong is a vowel sound which is made by running together two vowels.
2 The stress is generally on the last syllable of the word.

Back vowels	*Front vowels*
a as *u* in *cut*: akşam	**e** as *e* in *red*: reçel
ı as *e* in butter: ılık	**i** as *i* in *pin*: içmek
o as *o* in *cope*: çok	**ö** as French *deux* or German *Köln*: köpek
u as *oo* in *foot*: uzun	**ü** as French *tu* or German *über*: üzüm

Consonants (similar to English but with the following exceptions):

c as *j* in *jam*:	can
ç as *ch* in *child*:	çay
ğ prolongs any preceding vowel:	doğan
j as *su* in *pleasure*:	jiklet
ş as *sh* in *shoe*:	şeyler
v as *v* in *very*:	ve

AT THE AIRPORT

Arrival At Turkish airports, passport control and customs procedures are similar to those at other international airports. You should check your duty-free allowances before entering Turkey. Most Turkish airports have duty-free shops for both incoming and outgoing passengers. There are also currency exchanges for international transactions.

Look out for these signs: **Pasaport Kontrol** (Passport Control), **Bagajlar** (Baggage Collection), **Gümrük** (Customs), **Banka** (Bank), **Çıkış** (Exit).

Hava alanında karşılaşma/ Meeting at the airport

Daniel Daffin and his wife Jill arrive at İzmir Airport. Daniel is greeted by his Turkish agent Tarık Yarımcı.

Tarık: **İyi günler,** efendim! **Affedersiniz,** Bay Daffin **siz misiniz?**
Daniel: **Evet. Benim adım** Daniel Daffin.
Tarık: **Kendimi tanıştırayım.** Benim adım Tarık Yarımcı.
Daniel: Ah, iyi günler, Tarık Bey. **Tanıştığımıza memnum oldum.**
Tarık: Lütfen, bavullarınızı veriniz.
Daniel: Çok teşekkürler.

1

Greetings and introductions

İyi günler	Hello (lit. Good days)
efendim	sir, madam
Affedersiniz	Excuse me
Bay Daffin siz misiniz?	Are you Mr Daffin?
Evet/Hayır	Yes/No
Benim adım ...	My name is ...
Kendimi tanıştırayım	Let me introduce myself
Tanıştığımıza memnum oldum	Pleased to meet you
Bavullarınızı veriniz	Give me your suitcases

Polite words

lütfen	please
teşekkürler	thank you (lit. thanks)
çok teşekkürler	thank you very much
teşekkür ederim	I thank you
peki, pekala, tamam	OK
özür dilerim	I'm sorry

EXCHANGING GREETINGS AND INFORMATION

Aile ile tanışma/Meeting the family

Jill is greeted by Tarık's wife Neslihan and their son Cem.

Neslihan: Siz Bayan Daffin olmalısınız!
Jill: Evet. Benim adım Jill Daffin.
Neslihan: Benim adım Neslihan. Ve **işte** oğlumuz Cem. Türkiye'ye hoş geldiniz. **Nasılsınız?**
Jill: Hoş bulduk. **İyiyim, teşekkürler.**

Saying how you are

Siz Bayan Daffin olmalısınız!	You must be Mrs Daffin
İşte oğlumuz	This is our son
Türkiye'ye hoş geldiniz	Welcome to Turkey
Hoş bulduk	lit. We have found pleasure (said in reply to **Hoş geldiniz**)
Nasılsınız?	How are you?
İyiyim	I am well
Ya siz?	And you?
Ben de iyiyim	I'm fine too

Forms of address

In Turkey people generally shake hands each time they meet and also when saying goodbye. There are different ways of addressing people depending on how formal you need to be.

a) If their names are not known:

Bay or Efendim	Mr, sir
Bayan or Hanımefendi	Mrs, madam
Bayan or Küçük Hanım	Miss

b) If their names are known (formal and polite):

Bay Yarımcı	Mr Yarımcı
Bayan Akçapınar	Mrs Akçapınar
Bayan Daffin	Miss Daffin

c) If their first names are known (informal but polite):

Tarık Bey or **Tarık Beyefendi**	Mr Tarık
Nermin Hanım or **Nermin Hanımefendi***	Mrs Nermin

* This form of address can also be used for Miss.

Saying Hello ...

Merhaba	Hello (informal)
İyi günler	Good day/hello
İyi sabahlar (or **Günaydın**), **Efendim**	Good morning (to a man)
İyi akşamlar (or **Tünaydın**), **Hanımefendi**	Good evening (to a lady)
İyi geceler	Good night

... and Goodbye

In Turkish, the person who is leaving says:

Hoşça kalınız	Goodbye
Görüşmek üzere	See you later

Someone staying behind says:
'Güle güle' *literally* 'Go with laughter!'

3

Introducing your family

İşte	oğlumuz	This (here) is *our* son
	kızımız	daughter
	büyük kızımız	eldest daughter
	küçük kızımız	youngest daughter
	annemiz	mother
	babamız	father

annemiz   **babamız**   **oğlumuz**

	Nationalities	*Countries*	*Languages*
	English **İngiliz**	England **İngiltere**	English **İngilizce**
	Scottish **İskoçyalı**	Scotland **İskoçya**	
	Welsh **Galyalı**	Wales **Galler**	
	Irish **İrlandalı**	Ireland **İrlanda**	
	American **Amerikalı**	USA **Amerika**	American English **Amerikan İngilizcesi**
	Canadian **Kanadalı**	Canada **Kanada**	
	Austrian **Avusturyalı**	Austria **Avusturya**	German **Almanca**
	German **Alman**	Germany **Almanya**	German **Almanca**

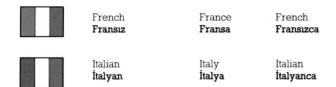

	French	France	French
	Fransız	**Fransa**	**Fransızca**
	Italian	Italy	Italian
	İtalyan	**İtalya**	**İtalyanca**

Language problems

Ben bir İngilizim	I am English
İngiltere' de yaşıyorum	I live in England
İngilizce konuşurum	I speak English
Lütfen yavaş konuşunuz	Please speak slowly
Sizi anlamıyorum	I don't understand you
Çok az Türkçe konuşurum	I speak very little Turkish
İngilizce bir gazeteniz var mı?	Do you have an English newspaper?

the way it works

People and things

Turkish nouns, adjectives and personal pronouns have no grammatical gender. **Plurals:** words are made plural by adding **-ler** or **-lar** to the singular form in accordance with the vowel harmony rule (see Introduction).
bavul (suitcase); bavul**lar** (suitcases)
gün (day); gün**ler** (days)

I am, you are, etc.

Verbs in Turkish usually go at the end of the phrase or sentence. Verb endings change according to the subject of the verb.

The equivalent of the English verb *to be* is **imek** in Turkish. It is a special verb with special uses.

Here is the present tense:

subject pronoun		*verb*		*subject pronoun*		*verb*	
ben ...		**im**	(I am)	**biz** ...		**iz**	(we are)
sen ...		**sin**	(you are, fam.)	**siz** ...		**siniz**	(you are)
o ...		**dir**	(he, she, it is)	**onlar** ...		**dirler**	(they are)

Ben bir İngiliz**im**	I am English
O Daniel Daffin**dir**	He is Daniel Daffin
Siz Bay Yarımcı**sınız**	You are Mr Yarımcı

Note The word for *you* in Turkish is normally **siz**, but with people you know well and members of the family use **sen**.

In Turkish two vowels cannot appear in succession, and when this would otherwise happen you insert the letter **-y-** between them:

Ben iyi**y**im I am well

Questions and negatives with imek

To put the verb in question form, insert -mi- (or its variations in accordance with the vowel harmony rule) before the verb ending.

Siz İngiliz misiniz?   Are you English?
Siz iyi misiniz?   Are you well?

If you want to make the sentence negative, insert -değil- before the verb ending:

Ben İngiliz değilim   I am not English
Ben iyi değilim   I am not well

things to do

1.1 Practise saying hello and goodbye to the following people:

1 Mr Oğuzkan (a business colleague)

2 Mr Engin (your local greengrocer)

3 Mrs Köylü (a friend of your mother)

4 Miss Yarımcı (a young girl)

1.2 Now practise greeting your friends:
1 Bay Yazıcı: Say hello and ask how he is.
2 Bayan Özveren: Say good morning.
3 Bayan Akçapınar: Say good evening and tell her you are
                        pleased to meet her.
4 Bayan Yarımcı: Say good day and ask how she is.

1.3 Your name is Mrs Ayşe and you meet Mr Oğuz and his friend in the street:

You: [Say hello to Mr Oğuz.]
Mr Oğuz: Merhaba, Bayan Ayşe, nasılsınız?
You: [Say thank you very much, you are fine. Ask how he is.]
Mr Oğuz: Teşekkürler. Ben de iyiyim. İşte Bayan Jale Erkmen.
You: [Say you are pleased to meet her and ask her how she is.]
Mrs Jale: Ben de iyiyim.

BOOKING A HOTEL ROOM

Accommodation   There are many types and categories of hotels (**otel**, **motel**), varying from the very basic to the luxurious with facilities such as private thermal baths, swimming-pools and air-conditioning. Detailed lists can be obtained from the local tourist information offices. Booking in advance is advisable, especially in the summer period, and you normally pay for the room per person.

You may be asked to fill out a registration form giving details of nationality (**milliyetiniz**), occupation (**mesleğiniz**), passport number (**pasaport numarası**), home address (**adresiniz**).

When travelling through the country, look out for signs **boş oda var** (Vacancies), **kiralık yazlık** (Holiday apartment to let), by the roadside or go to the nearest **Turizm Bürosu** (Tourist Information Office). There are also numerous **Pansiyon** (boarding houses) whose facilities and prices vary considerably.

Bir otel resepsiyonunda/
At the hotel reception

Daniel Daffin is checking in at the hotel Yunus.

Resepsiyoncu:	**İyi akşamlar,** efendim. Yardım edebilir miyim?
Daniel:	İyi akşamlar. **Biz, bir** hafta için, çift yataklı bir **oda ayırttık.**
Resepsiyoncu:	Adınız lütfen!
Daniel:	Adım Daniel Daffin.
Resepsiyoncu:	Bir dakika lütfen. Evet, Bay Daffin. Birinci katta oniki numaralı oda, efendim. İşte anahtarınız.
Daniel:	**Odada duş var mı?**
Resepsiyoncu:	Evet, duş ve tuvalet var.
Daniel:	**Ücreti ne kadar?**
Resepsiyoncu:	Sabah kahvaltısı dahil beş bin yedi yüz elli lira.
Daniel:	Pahalı değil.
Resepsiyoncu:	Lütfen şu kağıdı doldurunuz.
Daniel:	Teşekkürler.

At the hotel reception

Resepsiyoncu	Receptionist
İyi akşamlar	Good evening
Yardım edebilir miyim?	Can I help you?
Biz bir oda ayırttık	We have reserved a room
çift yataklı	double bed
Boş odanız var mı?	Do you have any vacant rooms?
Kaç gün için?	For how many days?
Bir/iki gün için	For a day/two days
Ben bir oda ayırttım	I have reserved a room
... **bir gece için**	... for one night
... **dört gece için**	... for four nights
... **bir hafta için**	... for a week
... **iki hafta için**	... for two weeks

Ben tek kişilik bir oda istiyorum	I would like a single room
... çift yataklı	... a double room
... iki tek yataklı	... with two single beds
... banyolu/duşlu	... with a bath/shower
... telefonlu	... with a telephone
... balkonlu	... with balcony
... ön/arka tarafta	... at the front/back
Adınız, lütfen	Your name please
Bir dakika lütfen	One minute please
Lütfen şu kağıdı doldurunuz	Please fill in that form

The room and the price

Birinci katta, ikinci katta	On the first floor, second floor
oniki numaralı	number twelve
İşte anahtarınız	Here is your key
sekiz numaralı odanın anahtarı	the key to room 8
Odada duş var mı?	Is there a shower in the room?
Evet, duş ve tuvalet var	Yes, a shower and a toilet
Telefon ve renkli televizyon var	There is a telephone and a colour television
Kaç lira?	How much?
Ücreti ne kadar?	What is the price?
... komple pansiyon olarak	... with full board
... yalnız kahvaltı dahil	... with breakfast only
Sabah kahvaltısı dahil	Breakfast included
beş bin yedi yüz elli lira	5,750 lira
Pahalı değil	It is not expensive

Paying the bill

Yarın ayrılıyorum	I am leaving tomorrow
Lütfen hesabı verirmisiniz?	Could I have the bill, please? (lit. Could you give me the bill)
Sanıyorum, ...	I think ...
... hesapta bir yanlışlık var	... there is a mistake in the bill
Kredi kartını kabul ediyor musunuz?	Do you accept credit-cards?
Her şey dahil mi?	Is everything included?

Numbers 1–10

0	1	2	3	4	5	6	7	8	9	10
sıfır	**bir**	**iki**	**üç**	**dört**	**beş**	**altı**	**yedi**	**sekiz**	**dokuz**	**on**

Note: When a noun follows a number, that noun is singular not plural, e.g.: iki bira/two beers   üç şarap/three wines   dört şişe ayran/four bottles of 'ayran'.
(**Şişe** means bottle and **ayran** is a drink made from yoghurt, water and salt.)

IN THE BAR

Otel barından bir içki/
A drink at the hotel bar

Garson: Buyurunuz efendim. Hoş geldiniz.
          Ne içmek istiyorsunuz?
Daniel: **Ben bir bira** içmek **istiyorum.**
Jill: Ben bir meyva suyu istiyorum.
Garson: Buyurunuz efendim, soğuk bir bira ve soğuk bir meyva
          suyu.
Daniel: **Ne kadar?**
Garson: Bin beş yüz altmış lira.
Daniel: İşte. (Hands him the money) Tamam mı?
Garson: Evet efendim. Teşekkürler, Siz nerelisiniz?
Jill: **Biz İngiliziz.** İngiltere'den geliyoruz.
Garson: Burada ne kadar kalacaksınız?
Daniel: Bir hafta kalacağız.
Garson: Çok güzel. İyi tatiller efendim.

Ordering a drink

Garson	Waiter
Buyurunuz	Come in, Welcome; Here it is
hoş geldiniz	welcome
ne içmek istiyorsunuz?	what do you want to drink?
Ben bira içmek istiyorum	I want to drink beer
şarap	wine
rakı	raki
meyva suyu	fruit juice
maden suyu	mineral water
çay	tea
kahve	coffee
soğuk bir bira	a cold beer
soğuk bir meyva suyu	a cold fruit juice
ne kadar?	how much?
beş bin yüz altmış lira	5,160 lira
İşte	Here it is
Tamam mı?	Is that OK?
Çok güzel	Very good

Saying where you are from

Siz nerelisiniz?	Where are you from?
Siz nereden geliyorsunuz?	Where do you come from?
Ben İngilizim	I am English
Ben Londra'dan geliyorum	I come from London

Useful words and phrases

ne kadar (süre, zaman)?	How long?
Burada ne kadar kalacaksınız?	How long are you staying here?
Bir hafta kalacağız	We are staying for a week
İyi tatiller	Have a good holiday

the way it works

How to form words

There are no separate words for prepositions such as *to*, *at*, *in*, *on*, *from* in Turkish. These words are represented by suffixes – endings which are added on to nouns and pronouns and called case endings.

We have already met several of these in the dialogues in this unit, e.g.:

Oda**da** duş var mı?	Is there a shower *in* the room? (**Oda** = room)
Ben İngiltere**'den** geliyorum	I come *from* England

There are six cases in Turkish, all of which take different sets of endings, except the nominative (subject) case which takes no ending. Don't be too concerned with the cases at the moment. They will be introduced gradually throughout the book.

11

There is/there are

Note the following example from the dialogue:

Odada duş **var mı**?	Is there a shower in the room?

The answer in this case is:

Evet, duş ve tuvalet **var**.	Yes, there is shower and toilet.

Adding **mı** turns the statement into a question.

Substituting **yok** means 'there isn't/there aren't'.

Odada havlular **yok**	There aren't any towels

Note: **var** is also used to mean 'to have' in the sense of availability.

Boş odanız var **mı**?	Are there any vacant rooms? (= do you have?)
Odada havlular var **mı**?	Are there any towels in the room?

Verbs

All Turkish verbs end in **-mek** or **-mak** in their infinitive form, in accordance with the vowel harmony rule (see Introduction). The part before the **-mek/-mak** is called the stem, e.g.:

ver**mek**	to give	bak**mak**	to look
iç**mek**	to drink	yaz**mak**	to write

The present tense

There are two forms of present tense in Turkish – the *aorist* and the *continuous present*. The *aorist* denotes continuing or habitual activity:

Sabahları çay içerim*   I drink tea in the mornings

*after consonant stems (**içmek** = to drink) a vowel is added before the **r**.

The *continuous present* is used for actions either in progress or envisaged and is differentiated by means of the suffix **-yor-** which is placed *after* the verb stem and *before* the ending:

Çay İçi**yor**um*   I *am drinking* tea

*after consonant stems a closed vowel is added before **-yor-**.

Endings of verbs

Different endings are added to the stem to indicate who the subject of the verb is. The vowel in the ending will be harmonised with the previous sound in accordance with the vowel harmony rule.

gel**mek** (to come)	*Continuous Present*
Ben İngiltere'den geliyor**um**	*I* come from England
Biz Fransa'dan geliyor**uz**	*We* came from France
Siz İtalya'dan geliyor**sunuz**	*You* come from Italy
Nereden geliyor**sunuz**?	Where do *you* come from?

How to say you want something

If you want something use the verb **istemek**.

Ne **istiyorsunuz**?	What do *you want*?
Bir bira **istiyorum**	*I want* a beer
Bir oda **istiyoruz**	*We want* a room
Ben İngiltere'ye telefon etmek **istiyorum**	*I want* to 'phone England

things to do

.4 Practise booking a room at a hotel.

Receptionist: İyi akşamlar efendim. Yardım edebilir miyim?
You: [Say good morning and ask if there are any vacant rooms.]
Receptionist: Evet, efendim. Kaç gün için?
You: [Say for a week.]
Receptionist: Bir dakika lütfen ...
You: [Say you would like a single room with a shower]
Receptionist: Özür dilerim. Çift yataklı bir oda var fakat tek kişilik yok.
You: [Say that's OK. Ask if there is a shower in the room]
Receptionist: Evet, efendim, duş ve tuvalet var.
You: [Say that's fine and ask how much it is.]

.5 You are in a taverna ordering drinks for your party. Everyone seems to want something different, so you can cope?

ORDERING BREAKFAST

Breakfast is usually a light meal consisting of bread, butter, white curd cheese, olives and jam, and is served with black Turkish tea. It is, however, possible to order a continental-style breakfast in larger hotels. Turkish coffee can also be served on request.

Otelde sabah kahvaltısı/
Breakfast at the hotel

Jill and Daniel are ordering breakfast.

Garson:	Günaydın, efendim, buyurunuz.
Jill:	**Günaydın.**
Daniel:	İyi sabahlar.
Garson:	Kahvaltı istiyor musunuz?
Daniel:	Evet, lütfen. Benim karnım çok aç.
Jill:	Kahvaltıda neler var?
Garson:	Ekmek, tereyağı, beyaz peynir, zeytin ve reçel var. Çay, kahve veya meyva suyu içebilirsiniz.
Daniel:	**Lütfen bana,** ekmek, tereyağı ve reçel **getiriniz. Ben bir** bardak Türk çayı içmek **istiyorum,** lütfen.
Jill:	Lütfen bana, ekmek, beyaz peynir, zeytin ve bir bardak mevya suyu getiriniz.
Garson:	Derhal efendim. Afiyet olsun.

14

What's for breakfast?

Kahvaltı	Breakfast
Kahvaltı istiyor musunuz?	Would you like breakfast?
Benim karnım çok aç	I am very hungry
Ben çok susadım	I am very thirsty
Kahvaltıda neler var?	What is there for breakfast?
ekmek	bread
tereyağı	butter
beyaz peynir	white-curd cheese
zeytin	olives
reçel	jam
çay	tea
Türk çayı	Turkish tea
kahve	coffee
Türk kahvesi	Turkish coffee
içebilirsiniz	you can drink
lütfen bana ... getiriniz	please bring me
bir bardak	a glass
Derhal, efendim	Immediately, sir
Afiyet olsun	Good appetite

AT THE RESTAURANT

Turkish cuisine is world-famous and a great experience. There are hot and cold dishes with olive oil, **meze** (starters), a great variety of fresh salads and fruits, and many kinds of fish from the Black Sea, the Aegean and the Mediterranean.

Bir lokantaya davet/Invitation to a restaurant

Jill and Daniel are met by their friends Recep and Tuncay who have invited them for a meal in a Turkish restaurant.

Garson: Buyurunuz efendim, hoş geldiniz.
Recep: **Şurada dört kişilik boş bir masa var.**
Jill: Bu lokanta çok temiz ve büyük.

Tuncay: Evet, yemekler de güzeldir.
Garson: Yemekten önce bir şey içer misiniz?
Daniel: İçecek neler var?
Garson: İşte liste, efendim.
Jill: Ben bir bardak limonata istiyorum.
Tuncay: Benim için soğuk bir kokakola lütfen.
Recep: Bir büyük bira lütfen.
Daniel: Bir bardak Doluca beyaz şarap lütfen.
Garson: Derhal efendim.
Jill: Türk yemekleri gerçekten çok leziz. Ben, bir yayla çorbası, **bir porsiyon** Adana şiş kebabı ve cacık istiyorum.
Tuncay: Ben, çoban salatası, zeytin yağlı taze fasulye ve İskender kebabı istiyorum.
Recep: Karışık salata, yaprak sarması ve ıspanaklı börek getiriniz.
Daniel: Cacık, pilav ve İnegöl köftesi lütfen.
Garson: **Yemekte içki ister misiniz?**
Recep: Evet, 1977 Doluca kırmızı ve bir küçük rakı lütfen.
Garson: Derhal efendim. Afiyet olsun.

Booking a table

Şurada boş bir masa var	There's a vacant table over there
burada/orada/şurada	here/over there/there
boş/dolu	empty (vacant)/full (occupied)
Dört kişilik bir masanız var mı?	Do you have a table for four?
pencere yanında/terasta/ köşede	by the window/on the terrace/ in the corner
Bir masa ayırtmak istiyorum	I'd like to reserve a table
temiz/kirli	clean/dirty
büyük/küçük	big (large)/small
restoran/lokanta	restaurant
yemekler	dishes

Ordering a meal

Yemekten önce bir şey içer misiniz?	Would you like to drink something before the meal?
önce/sonra	before/after
İçecek neler var?	What is there to drink?
İşte liste	Here is the list
İşte yemek listesi	Here is the menu

DOĞU İŞKEMBECİSİ VE LOKANTASI

PİLAVLAR		TATLILAR	
Pirinç pilav T yağlı	......	Fırın sütlaç	......
Bulgur pilav	......	Keşkül	......
İç pilav	......	Aşure	......
Patlıcan pilav	......	Ekmek kadayıfı	......
Bezelyeli pilav	......		
Meyhane pilavı	......	Kemal Paşa	......
Fırın makarna	......	İrmik helvası	......
Kıymalı Makarna	......		
....	......	Tel kadayıf	......
BÖREKLER		Revani	
Kıymalı börek	......	Kabak tatlısı cevizli	......
Peynirli börek	......	Çilek komposto	......
Ispanaklı börek	......	Elma komposto	......
ZEYTİNYAĞLILAR		Elma komposto	......
~~ıt ciğeri		A~~~	

bir bardak Doluca beyaz şarap	a glass of Doluca white wine
gerçekten	as a matter of fact
leziz	tasty
bir porsiyon ...	a portion of ...
Türk yemekleri	Turkish food
yayla çorbası	a kind of yoghurt soup
Adana şiş kebabı	Adana-style skewered kebab
cacık	cucumber slices in yoghurt with garlic and salt
çoban salatası	shepherd's salad
zeytin yağlı taze fasulye	green beans in olive oil
İskender kebabı	döner kebab with yoghurt and tomato sauce, cooked in butter

17

yaprak sarması	stuffed vine leaves
ıspanaklı börek	pastry with spinach
pilav	plain cooked rice
İnegöl köftesi	meat-balls cooked in İnegöl style
Yemekte içki ister misiniz?	Would you like a drink with your meal?
Tavsiye ederim ...	I recommend ...
Etyemez yemekleri var mı?	Are there any vegetarian dishes?
Ne arzu edersiniz, et mi yoksa balık mı?	What would you like, meat or fish?

Paying the bill

Hesabı getirir misiniz?	Will you bring the bill?
Kredi kartı ile ödeyebilir miyim?	Can I pay by credit-card?
Servis dahil mi?	Is service included?
Tuvaletler nerede?	Where are the toilets?
Yemekler çok nefisti	The food was excellent

Table vocabulary

bıçak	knife	**peçete**	napkin
çatal	fork	**kürdan**	toothpick
kaşık	spoon	**tuz**	salt
tabak	plate	**biber**	pepper
bardak	glass	**acı biber**	hot pepper (cayenne)
kültablası	ashtray	**kara biber**	black pepper

the way it works

A polite command

Look at the following example from the dialogue:

Lütfen, **bana** ekmek ... **getiriniz**   Please bring me some bread
Lütfen, **bana** hesabı **getiriniz**   Please bring me the bill

This imperative form is very easy to learn: **getiriniz** comes directly from the stem of the verb, in this case **getir-**, to which the ending **-(i)niz** is added.

Lütfen, **bana** ... **veriniz**   Please give me

Note the position of **bana** (to me) which always goes before the verb.

This and that, here and there

Bu lokanta	this restaurant	**burada**	here
Şu masa	that table	**şurada**	there
O masa	that table over there	**orada**	over there

things to do

2.1 You are with a group of tourists at a Turkish hotel and the only person who can speak the language. The waiter asks **'Ne arzu edersiniz?'** (What would you like?). Can you order breakfast for everyone?

1 Frances: bread, white curd cheese and a cup of Turkish coffee.

2 Peter: bread, butter and jam.

3 Andrew: bread, olives and fruit juice.

4 Jane: bread, jam and Turkish coffee.

  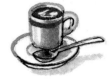

2.2 You have arrived at a restaurant. Can you tell the waiter what you want.
1 Ask if there is a table for four.
2 Ask the waiter to bring you the menu.
3 Ask what there is to drink.
4 Say you would like a soup, one shish kebab, one Adana kebab with a mixed salad.
5 Ask for a bottle of raki.
6 Ask for the bill.

SHOPPING FOR FOOD

Money   The monetary system in Turkey is the Turkish Lira (TL).
The system is decimal. No limit is imposed on the amount of foreign
currency taken into Turkey, but not more than the equivalent of
1,000 US Dollars in Turkish Lira can be taken out of Turkey. In
most tourist areas major credit cards are accepted.

Shops are generally open from 8.30 am to 1 pm and from 2 pm to
7 pm, and close on Sundays except in tourist areas where they
can be open from early morning until midnight or beyond.

There are local markets on specific days of the week for each
district, where one can buy fresh food, fruit and vegetables and other
requirements.

Pazarda alış-veriş/Shopping at the market

Daniel and Jill are at the local market.

Daniel:	Bak, şurada çok güzel şeftaliler var. Biraz satın alalım.
Satıcı:	Buyurunuz. Ne kadar istiyorsunuz?
Jill:	**İki kilo lütfen.**
Daniel:	**Kaç lira?**
Satıcı:	Kilosu 750 lira beyim.
Daniel:	İşte 1500 liranız.
Satıcı:	Teşekkürler, afiyetle yiyiniz.

Buying food

Biraz satın alalım	Let's buy some
Ne kadar istiyorsunuz?	How much do you want?
lütfen iki kilo	Two kilos please
Kaç lira?	How much (does it cost)?
Kilosu 750 lira	750 lira per kilo
Afiyetle yiyiniz	Eat it with good appetite

Useful shopping phrases

bir litre	a litre of
iki dilim	two slices of
bir paket	a packet of ...
fazla/az/çok fazla	more/less/too much
bu/şu	this one/that one
bunlar/şunlar	these/those
yarım kilo	half a kilo
250 gram	250 grams
Başka?	Anything else?
Hepsi bu kadar, teşekkürler	That's all, thanks

SHOPPING FOR PRESENTS

It is advisable to bargain politely over the price of large items like carpets and leather goods.

Carpets, kilims, onyx, china, leather, copperware, silk, towelling, herbs and spices are good items to purchase for value and quality.

21

Hediyelik eşya dükkanında/
At the souvenir shop

While out window-shopping, Jill and Daniel are invited into a shop by Cüneyt, the shopkeeper.

Cüneyt: Buyurunuz efendim! Hoş geldiniz! Satın almak önemli değil. Bakınız!
Daniel: Teşekkürler.
Jill: **Bu nedir?**
Cüneyt: **O bir semaverdir.** Belki biliyorsunuz, biz Türkler çayı çok severiz.
Daniel: **Biz** küçük bir kilim **satın almak istiyoruz.**
Cüneyt: Burada pek çok çeşitimiz var. Pahalı, ucuz. İpek, pamuk ipliği veya yün elde dokunmuş!
Jill: Şu küçük mavi ve kırmızı motifli kilimi **görebilir miyim?**
Cüneyt: Buyurunuz, güzel bir yörük kilimi!
Jill: Kaç lira?
Cüneyt: Pahalı değil. 150,000 liradır. Değerli ve hakiki bir el sanatı.
Daniel: 125,000 lira verebiliriz!
Cüneyt: Peki sizin için 130,000 lira.
Daniel: **Peki, işte paranız.**
Cüneyt: Teşekkürler. Güle güle eskitiniz.

Buying souvenirs

satın almak	to buy
önemli değil	it is not important/essential
Bakınız	Please look (at)
Bu nedir?	What is this?
O bir semaverdir	It is a samovar
Belki biliyorsunuz	Perhaps you know
biz Türkler severiz	we, the Turks, like ...
küçük bir kilim	a small rug
Burada	In here
pek çok çeşitimiz	a lot of different kinds
pahalı/ucuz	expensive/cheap
ipek/pamuk/yün	silk/cotton/wool
elde dokunmuş	hand-woven
eski/yeni	old/new
büyük/küçük	big/small
beyaz/siyah/mavi	white/black/blue
yeşil/sarı/kırmızı	green/yellow/red
kahve rengi/pembe/gri	brown/pink/grey
motifli	patterned
... görebilir miyim?	Can I see ... ?
güzel bir yörük kilimi	a pretty Turcoman rug
değerli ve hakiki	valuable and original
bir el sanatı	a handmade piece
... lira verebiliriz	we can give ... lira!

Peki sizin için ... lira?	O.K. for you ... lira
Güle güle eskitiniz	Please make use of it with happiness.
bir seramik tabak	a pottery dish
bir kaç tesbih (taşı)	worry beads
bir gömlek	a shirt

the way it works

Adjectives

Adjectives in Turkish are placed before the noun, as in English:

küçük kilim	small rug
taze meyva lar	fresh fruits

When the indefinite article **bir** precedes the adjective, it makes the noun indefinite but when the adjective precedes the indefinite article, the noun becomes definite:

bir küçük kilim	a small rug
küçük bir kilim	the small rug
değerli ve hakiki bir halı	the valuable and genuine carpet

To be able to ...

Look at the following phrase:

Çay veya kahve içebilirsiniz   You can drink tea or coffee

To say *you can* you add **-ebil-** or **-abil-** to the stem of the verb before the tense and personal suffixes.

125,000 lira ver**ebil**iriz   We can give 125,000 lira

Following the same pattern:

görmek (to see)   gör**ebil**mek (to be able to see)

Here is the aorist present tense of **görebilmek**:

görebilirim	I can see	görebiliriz	we can see
görebilirsin	you can see	görebilirsiniz	you can see
görebilir	he/she can see	görebilirler	they can see

NB it is also possible to use the simple present tense with **-ebil-/-abil**:
gör**ebil**iyorum   *lit.* I am being able to see

To ask a question (e.g. 'Can I see?') insert the suffix **-mi-** before the personal suffix, not forgetting to put a **y** between the vowels:

görebilir miyim?	Can I see?
bakabilir miyiz?	Can we look?

Accusative case

If the object of the verb is non-specific you do not need to add any suffix:

Biz küçük bir kilim istiyoruz	We want a small carpet
Biz elma istiyoruz	We want an apple

However, if the object of the verb is specific and a single word you have to add -(y)i- as an accusative suffix.

Şu küçük kilimi görebilir miyiz?   Can we see that small carpet?
Biz elmayı istiyoruz?   We want the apple

If the object of the verb is specific and a compound word, it will take -(n)i- as one of the accusative suffixes after the coupling suffix:

Biz şu küçük **yörük kilimini** istiyoruz   We want that small *Turcoman rug*
(Here, the first i added to kilim stems from coupling, but the second i is the accusative suffix preceded by the liaison letter **n**.) (See Saturday, page 61 for further details.)

Here is the full pattern of endings for the accusative case:

Last vowel of word	Suffix -(y)i-
a, ı	-(y)i
o, u	-(y)u
e, ı	-(y)i
ö, ü	-(y)ü

things to do

2.3 You are in the market buying fruit for a picnic. You like the look of the peaches (**şeftaliler**) and the grapes (**üzüm**) and you also want some tomatoes (**domates**).

You: [Say you'd like a kilo of grapes.]
Shopkeeper: Peki. Başka bir şey, hanımefendi?
You: [Say those peaches look good. Ask how much they are.]
Shopkeeper: Kilosu 600 lira.
You: [Say you'd like a kilo, please.]
Shopkeeper: Başka bir şey?
You: [Ask for half a kilo of tomatoes.]
Shopkeeper: Başka bir şey?
You: [Say no, that's all and ask how much it comes to.]

2.4 You have been given a shopping list in Turkish. Can you work out what you are in fact buying?

> 200 gram beyaz peynir.
> 1 ekmek
> 1 litre süt.
> 1 paket çay
> yarım kilo pirinç
> 250 gram zeytin

2.5 You are buying presents for the family. Can you ask for the following:

1 a small blue rug   4 some worry beads
2 a samovar   5 a white shirt
3 a large pottery dish

Sabahleyin

PUBLIC TRANSPORT

There are scheduled internal flights linking major cities. The service is efficient and reasonably priced.

Travelling by **train** may be tiring but is an excellent way to see the country. It is comfortable and inexpensive. Express services are also available.

Intercity **bus** services are by far the best means of travel. They are comfortable, extraordinarily cheap and reliable, with a superb network.

Taxi fares are reasonable but should be agreed upon before making the journey as there is no control on the prices except in big cities like İstanbul or Ankara. Private car hire is available but is not cheap.

The common taxi 'dolmuş' is a great favourite. These are usually licensed private cars or minibuses with specific routes calling at recognised stops. The destination is written on the top of the front window. Fares are fixed and collected en route.

Dolmuş durağı nerededir?/
Where is the dolmuş stop?

Jill and Daniel want to go to the town centre. They ask Tarık how to get there.

Jill: Affedersiniz! **Biz** şehir merkezine **gitmek istiyoruz.**
           Buradan oraya **nasıl gidebiliriz**?
Tarık: Buradan Merkez dolmuşları ile gidebilirsiniz.
Jill: **Dolmuş durağı nerededir?**
Tarık: Sağda ikinci sokakta, köşe başında.
Jill: Teşekkürler. Haydi gidelim.
They arrive at the dolmuş stop
Dolmuşcu: Merkez! Merkez! Hemen gidecek. Buyurunuz!
Jill: **Merkez, lütfen. Kaç lira?**
Dolmuşcu: Bir kişi 750 lira, bayan.
Jill: İşte 2000 lira.
Dolmuşcu: Buyurunuz 500 liranız.

Finding your way

Affedersiniz	Excuse me
şehir merkezine	to the city centre
Buradan oraya	From here to there
... nasıl gidebiliriz?	How do we get to ...?

Hava alanına nasıl giderim?	How do I get to the airport?
İstasyon(a)/liman(a) ...	... to the station/to the harbour
... ile gidebilirsiniz	... you can go by/on
Merkez dolmuşları	by dolmuş with destination 'Centre'
... nerededir?	Where is ...?
Dolmuş durağı nerededir?	Where is the dolmuş stop?
sağ/sol	right/left
sağda	on the right
solda	on the left
Sağda ikinci sokakta ...	The second street on the right
... köşe başında	... on the corner
Sola sapınız	Turn left (**sapmak** – to turn)
Bu sokaktan doğru gidiniz	Go down the street
dosdoğru	straight on
Bu yoldan dosdoğru gidiniz	Go straight on
dörtyolda/ışıklarda	at the crossroads/at the lights
ileride/karşıda	over there/opposite
pazarın arkasında	behind the market
caminin yanında	near the mosque

Other useful phrases

Haydi gidelim	Let's go
Hemen gidecek	It's going immediately!
Kaç lira?	How much is it?
Bir kişi	one person
Bana yardım eder misiniz?	Can you help me?
yakındır/uzaktır	it is near/far
Plaj ne kadar uzaktır?	How far is the beach?
yaklaşık	about
Yaklaşık 200 kilometredir	It's about 200 km.
Yaklaşık 300 metre sağdadır	It's about 300 metres on the right
Biraz karışık	It's a little confusing!
Sizin bir haritanız var	You have a street map
Biz buradayız	We are here
İşte Hayat sokağı	This is Hayat street
Evet. Anladım	Yes. I did understand
Dolmuş bizi oraya dosdoğru götürecekmi?	Will the dolmuş take us there direct?
Kuşadası'ndan Efes'e gitmek ne kadar sürer?	How long does it take to get from Kuşadası to Ephesus?

Means of transport

dolmuş	shared taxi	**tren**	train
taksi	taxi	**uçak**	plane
otobüs	bus, coach	**feribot**	ferry
minibüs	minibus	**belediye otobüsü**	public bus
Yürüyerek gidebilirsiniz	You can go on foot		

27

Bir minibüs yolculuğu/Travel by minibus

Later that morning Jill and Daniel decide to travel from Yalova to Termal by minibus.

Jill:	**Affedersiniz,** Termal **minibüsleri nereden kalkıyor?**
Yaya:	**Solda** ikinci sokak başında.
Daniel:	Teşekkürler.
Şöför:	Buyurun bayım. Termal'e.
Jill:	Ne zaman hareket ediyorsunuz?
Şöför:	On dakika içinde, hanımefendi.
Daniel:	İki kişi kaç lira?
Şöför:	2000 lira bayım.
Daniel:	İşte buyurun. Biz Termal'e gelince lütfen indiriniz.
Şöför:	Merak etme beyim.

Asking for information

... minibüsleri nereden kalkıyor?	Where do the ... minibuses go from?
Solda ikinci sokak başında	at the corner of the second street on the left
Ne zaman hareket ediyorsunuz?	When do you go?
On dakika içinde	In ten minutes
İki kişi kaç lira?	How much for two people?
Bizi Termal'e gelince lütfen indiriniz	Please tell us to get off at Termal
Merak etmeyiniz	Don't worry

the way it works

Question words

Banka **nerede(dir)?**	*Where is* the bank?
Postahane **nerededir?**	*Where is* the post-office?
Otel **nasıl**(dır)?	*What is* the hotel *like*
yemek	the meal
yol	the road
... **nasıl** giderim?	*How* do I get to ...?
Ne kadar sürer?	*How long* does it take?
Ne zaman hareket ediyorsunuz?	*When* do you set off?
Ne zaman açıktır/kapalıdır?	*When* is it open/closed?
Kaç lira?	*How much* is it?

Understanding the time

(for a list of numbers see page 9)
Saat kaç?   What is the time?

The reference points for telling the time are the hour and the half-hour:
a) when the time is *after* the hour or half-hour; **-geçiyor** is used:
Saat ikiyi on **geçiyor**   It is ten past two

b) when time is *before* the hour or half-hour, **-var** is used;
Saat dörde beş **var**   It is five to four

The most important things to remember are:

Saat on	It is ten o'clock
saat onu on geçiyor	It is ten past ten
saat onu çeyrek geçiyor	It is quarter past ten
saat on buçuk	It is half past ten
saat ona on var	It is ten to ten
saat ona çeyrek var	It is quarter to ten

If you cannot remember all of these, you can still read the time on a
24-hour digital basis:
on kırk   10.40   yirmi kırk   20.40
Saat on dört otuz altı   It is 14.36
Check the numbers on page 9.

To ask at what time something will happen:

a) To fix a time *after* the hour or half-hour, **-geçe** is used:
Saat kaçta gelecekler?   What time will they come?
Saat biri çeyrek **geçe** gelecekler   They'll come at quarter past one

b) To fix a time *before* the hour or half-hour, **-kala** is used:
Saat kaçta dönecekler?   What time will they return?
Saat dörde on **kala** dönecekler   They return at ten to four

To ask at what time the bus/train/dolmuş/passenger-boat or ferry leaves
you say:
Otobüs/Tren/Dolmuş/Vapur/Feribot **ne zaman hareket ediyor?** or **ne zaman kalkıyor?**

İstanbul'a tren **ne zaman hareket ediyor?**	What time does the train leave for İstanbul?
Emirgan'a vapur **ne zaman kalkıyor?**	What time does the passenger-boat leave for Emirgan?

And to find out what time it arrives:
Otobüs **ne zaman varacak?**   When will the bus arrive?
Vapur **ne zaman varacak?**   When will the passenger-boat arrive?

Here are the names of some places you may find useful:

istasyon/gar	station	**banka**	bank
postahane	post-office	**hava alanı**	airport
enformasyon bürosu	information	**liman**	harbour
cami	mosque	**çarşı**	market
otobüs terminali	bus-station	**stadyum**	stadium
vilayet konağı	town-hall	**karakol**	police-station
kale	castle	**müze**	museum
park/çocuk bahçesi	park		

29

CARŞAMBA Sabahleyin WEDNESDAY

things to do

3.1 Can you ask a passer-by:
1 where the post-office is
2 where the tourist information office is
3 where the Osman Paşa Caddesi is
4 where the railway station is.

3.2 Now ask the person how you get to:
1 the castle **3** the museum
2 the harbour **4** the mosque

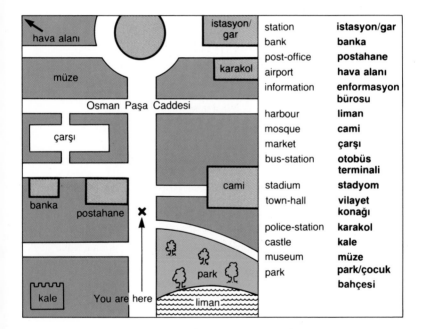

station	**istasyon/gar**
bank	**banka**
post-office	**postahane**
airport	**hava alanı**
information	**enformasyon bürosu**
harbour	**liman**
mosque	**cami**
market	**çarşı**
bus-station	**otobüs terminali**
stadium	**stadyom**
town-hall	**vilayet konağı**
police-station	**karakol**
castle	**kale**
museum	**müze**
park	**park/çocuk bahçesi**

3.3 You are at point X on the map and you overhear someone giving a tourist some simple directions. Can you interpret for him and say where he is going to?
1 Bu yoldan doğru gidiniz, sonra sağdaki ilk sokağa sapınız. Cami oradadır.
2 Bu yoldan doğru gidiniz. Soldaki ilk sokağa sapınız. Postahane orada, köşededir.
3 Bu yoldan dosdoğru gidiniz. Yolun sonunda, sağda istasyon var.

30

TICKETS AND INFORMATION

At the coach terminal you will find many companies operating to and from the same destinations. You can choose any one of them, but as a general rule use the most reputable ones since their services are more reliable.

When buying tickets check the destination, departure time, seat numbers and the number of the departure platform. As travelling gets very busy in the tourist season, the terminals become extremely crowded, so watch out for your belongings and make sure that you are on the right bus for your destination.

Bursa-Uludağ'a iki bilet/
Two tickets to Bursa-Uludağ

Jill and Daniel are buying tickets to Bursa-Uludağ from a company named **Bursanın Gülü** (The rose of Bursa).

Jill: İyi günler. **Biz** Bursa-Uludağ'a **gitmek istiyoruz.**
Katip: Hangi gün, ne zaman?
Daniel: **Yarın sabah.**
Katip: Bir dakika, kaç kişilik?
Jill: **İki kişi için.**
Katip: Evet, boş yerimiz var, **saat sabah dokuz buçukta.**
Daniel: **Bir bilet ne kadar?**
Katip: Bir kişi **yalnız gidiş** 3,500 liradır. Bir kişi **gidiş-dönüş** 6,800 liradır.

31

Jill: Biz iki kişilik gidiş-dönüş bileti istiyoruz.
Katip: Peki, adınız?
Daniel: Bay ve bayan Daffin.
Katip: İşte biletleriniz.
Jill: İşte 13,600 liranız.
Katip: Teşekkürler. Lütfen terminale bir saat önce geliniz. Görüşmek üzere, iyi günler.
Daniel: Teşekkürler, hoşça kalınız.

Buying tickets for the coach

Ne zaman?	What time?
Hangi gün	Which day?
yarın sabah	Tomorrow morning
bir dakika	one minute
Kaç kişilik?	For how many persons?
boş yerimiz var, saat sabah dokuz buçukta	We have vacant seats at 9.30 am
Bir bilet ne kadar?	How much is a ticket?
yalnız gidiş	one way
gidiş-dönüş bileti	return ticket
işte biletleriniz	Here are your tickets
terminale bir saat önce geliniz	Come to the terminal one hour beforehand
Görüşmek üzere	See you later
hoşça kalınız	Goodbye

Entry tickets

Jill and Daniel are at the incredible calcium springs of Pamukkale where the water petrifies as it cascades down the hill, leaving the landscape encrusted with extraordinarily shaped layers of mineral deposits.

As well as the Aphrodisias and Hierapolis ruins, visiting Pamukkale is a must!

Bir bilet ne kadar?/How much is a ticket?

Jill and Daniel are going to the swimming-pool at the top of the hill.

Gişe memuru: Buyurunuz, efendim.
Jill: Biz havuzda yüzmek istiyoruz. Kaç lira?
Gişe memuru: Bir saat için 3,000 lira, bir kişi için.
Daniel: Biz iki saat kalacağız. İşte 12,000 liranız.
Gişe memuru: İşte biletleriniz. İçeride soyunma odaları var. Lokanta veya büfeyi kullanabilirsiniz. Su çok sıcak gelebilir, lütfen uzun süre kalmayınız. İyi eğlenceler.
Daniel: Hierapolis harabeleri yakında mıdır?
Gişe memuru: Bu yolun solundan gidiniz. Hemen göreceksiniz.

Buying tickets for the swimming-pool

gişe memuru	ticket officer
Biz havuzda yüzmek istiyoruz	We want to swim in the pool
Bir saat için	For an hour
biz iki saat kalacağız	We'll stay for two hours
soyunma odaları	changing-rooms
Lokanta veya büfeyi kullanabilirsiniz	You can use the restaurant or snack-bar
Su çok sıcak gelebilir	The water may seem to be very hot
Lütfen uzun süre kalmayınız	Please do not stay in too long
İyi eğlenceler	Have a good time
harabeler yakında mıdır?	Are the ruins nearby?
Bu yolun solundan gidiniz	Go along this street to the left
Hemen göreceksiniz	You'll see it at once

the way it works

Adverbs of time

şimdi	now	henüz	yet, still
sonra	later	derhal, hemen	at once
bugün	today	erken	early
dün	yesterday	geç	late
yarın	tomorrow	önce	before
bu sabah	this morning	sonunda	finally
ertesi gün	the following day	o zaman	then
evvelki gün	the day before	geçen hafta	last week
arasıra	now and then	bazen	sometimes
çabucak	quickly	yavaşça	slowly

Adverbs of place

içeri	inside	yukarı	up
dışarı	outside	aşağı	down
ileri	forwards	karşı	opposite
geri	backwards		

Locative case endings

You may have noticed in the previous dialogue the phrase:

Biz **havuzda** yüzmek istiyoruz   We want to swim *in the* pool

This is an example of the locative case which is used in Turkish to express the prepositions *at*, *in* and *on*. The endings depend on the vowel harmony rule and are either **-de/-da** or **-te/-ta** (after the consonants ç, f, h, k, p, s, ş, t).

Here is the full pattern of endings:

last vowel of word	locative suffix
a, ı, o, u	-da or -ta
e, i, ö, ü	-de or -te

Here are some further examples:
otelde   in the hotel   masada   on the table

things to do

.4   You want to go to the Hittite museum (Hitit Müzesi) on the slope of the old citadel of Ankara. You stop a passer-by to ask how to get there.

You:	[Say you want to go to the Hittite Museum and ask how to get there.]
Passer-by:	Neresi ... Ah, buradan dolmuşlarla gidebilirsiniz.
You:	[Ask where the dolmuş stop is.]
Passer-by:	Bu yoldan doğru gidiniz. Sağda ikinci sokak başında dolmuş durağı vardır.
You:	[Ask whether the dolmus will take you direct.]
Passer-by:	Evet, müze yolun tam karşısındadır.
You:	[Say thank you very much.]
Passer-by:	Bir şey değil.

.5   **a)** You are at the coach station with a party of tourists all of whom want to go to different places. Can you ask at what time the coaches leave for their various destinations. (Efes, İzmir, Bodrum, Kuşadası)?

b) Now, can you understand the answers? Here are the times in English. Can you say what they would have been in Turkish?

	HAREKET	
İstanbul – Efes	9.10	14.00
İstanbul – İzmir	9.30	15.20
İstanbul – Bodrum	10.00	17.45
İstanbul – Kuşadası	10.40	20.15

c) Can you also ask at what time each one will arrive.

3.6 You are making enquiries about coaches to Kuşadası.

You:	[Say you want to go to Kuşadası.]
Clerk:	Hangi gün, ne zaman?
You:	[Say this morning.]
Clerk:	Kaç kişilik?
You:	[Say for two people.]
Clerk:	Evet, boş yerimiz var, saat sabah onbir buçukta.
You:	[Ask how much the ticket is.]
Clerk:	Yalnız gidiş 7,500 lira, bir gidiş-dönüş bileti 15,000 lira.
You:	[Say two single tickets, please.]
Clerk:	Peki, adınız?
You:	[Give your name.]
Clerk:	İşte biletleriniz.
You:	[Say here is 15,000 lira and thank him.]

AT THE BANK

Banks are open from Monday to Saturday, from 8.30 am to 12 noon and from 1.30 to 5 in the afternoon. Currency exchange bureaux (**Kambiyo**) at frontiers, stations, airports and popular tourist places are generally open outside banking hours.

Most European credit cards are valid with a passport. Travellers cheques and Eurocheques with the relevant cards and identification are also accepted. The Turkish currency is lira and you should hold on to your exchange slips when changing your Turkish liras back to your own currency.

Bir seyehat çeki bozdurmak istiyorum/ I'd like to cash a traveller's cheque

Jill wants to buy some Turkish pottery from the state monopoly shop (**Sümerbank Satış Mağazası**), but first they have to change some money at the bank.

Kambiyo memuru:	İyi günler. Ne arzu ediyorsunuz?
Daniel:	İyi günler. **Ben bir seyehat çeki bozdurmak istiyorum.**
Kambiyo memuru:	Peki, pasaportunuz lütfen.
Daniel:	Ah, işte buyurunuz.
Kambiyo memuru:	Ne kadar bozduracaksınız?
Daniel:	**100 sterlin karşılığı.**
Kambiyo memuru:	Lütfen şurayı imzalayınız.
Daniel:	**Bugün döviz kuru nedir?**

37

Kambiyo memuru:	2,400 Türk lirası, efendim.
Jill:	**Ben** de 36 sterlin **değiştirmek istiyorum.**
Kambiyo memuru:	Lütfen isminiz, adresiniz ve pasaport numaranız. Şurayı imzalayınız. İşte paralarınız, iyi günler.
Jill:	Teşekkürler.

Changing money

banka memuru	bank clerk
Kambiyo memuru	exchange clerk
Ne arzu ediyorsunuz?	What would you like?
Bir seyehat çeki bozdurmak istiyorum	I'd like to cash a traveller's cheque
Avrupa seyehat çeklerimi bozdurabilir miyim?	Can I cash my Eurocheques?
Ne kadar bozduracaksınız?	How much are you going to change?
100 sterlin karşılığı	Equivalent of £100 sterling
Lütfen şurayı imzalayınız	Please sign here
Bugün döviz kuru nedir?	What is the exchange-rate today?
Ben 36 sterlin değiştirmek istiyorum	I want to change £36 sterling in cash
isminiz, adresiniz ve pasaport numaraniz	Your name, your address and your passport number
İşte paralarınız	Here is your money

Other useful phrases

Ne kadar yapıyor?	What does it come to?
vezneye gidiniz	Go to the cash desk
Onlar size ödemeyi yapacaklar	They'll give you the money
paralar	money
İngiliz sterlini	English pounds
Amerikan doları	US dollars
Alman markı	German marks
ödemek	to pay
para yatırmak	to deposit
para çekmek	to withdraw

İngiliz sterlinim var	I have cash in pounds sterling
Çek kartım var	I have a cheque card
Banka kartım	a bank card
Kredi kartım	a credit card

the way it works

Genitive case

The genitive case is used when you want to say *of* or *'s*. Here is the full
pattern of the genitive suffixes.

last vowel of word	*genitive suffix*
a, ı	(n)ın
o, u	(n)un
e, i	(n)in
ö, ü	(n)ün

Here are some examples:

araba**nın**	of the car	Ankara**nın**	of Ankara
Cem**in**	Cem's	otel**in**	of the hotel

How to say My, Your, etc.

Look at the following phrase from the dialogue:

Lütfen ismin**iz**, adresin**iz** ve pasaport numaran**ız**.
Your name, your address and your passport number, please.

These endings (which follow the vowel harmony rule) are examples of the possessive, and may also occur with a personal pronoun in the *genitive* case as follows.

personal pronoun	word ending in a vowel	a consonant		
ben**im**	çanta**m**	bilet**im**	my	handbag/ticket
sen**in**	çanta**n**	bilet**in**	your	handbag/ticket
on**un**	çanta**sı**	bilet**i**	his/her	handbag/ticket
biz**im**	bile**piniz**	bilet**imiz**	our	handbag/ticket
siz**in**	çanta**nız**	bile**iniz**	your	handbag/ticket
onlar**ın**	çanta**ları**	bilet**leri**	their	handbag/ticket

Here are some other examples:

ben**im** bavul**um**	my suitcase	biz**im** oda**mız**	our room
sen**in** bilet**in**	your ticket	siz**in** ad**ınız**	your name
on**un** pasaport**u**	her passport	onlar**ın** araba**ları**	their car
benim seyehat çekler**im**	my travellers cheques		

Simple future tense

Ne kadar bozduracaksınız?   How much are you going to change?
                                    (**bozdurmak** – to change)

This is an example of the simple future tense which, as in English, is used to express intention. The suffix **-ecek/-acak** is inserted between the verb stem and the ending.

Note: The letter **k** between vowels becomes **ğ**. After a stem ending in a vowel the letter **y** is inserted. If the final vowel of the stem is **a** or **e** it is narrowed to **-ı** or **-i** by the subsequent **y**.

Here are some examples:
gideceğim   I'll go (**gitmek** – to go)
satın alacağız   I'll buy (**satın almak** – to buy)

The negative form of this tense is formed by inserting **-mı** or **-mi** between the stem and the tense suffix (satın al**mı**yacağım – I won't buy). The interrogative is formed by inserting **-mı** or **-mi** after the tense suffix and before the verb ending (satın alacak **mı**sınız? – will you buy?).

Some independent prepositions

As we have seen, many English prepositions are represented in Turkish by means of the case endings (e.g. *at*, *in* and *on* – locative case). However, there are some prepositions which are independent of the verb in Turkish as in English.

Here are some examples:

ile, -le, –la (with, by means of): Araba **ile** gidiyoruz (We are going *by* car)
için (*for*) İki gün **için** (*for* two days)
gibi (*like*) uçak **gibi** (*like* an aeroplane)
kadar (*as … as*) senin **kadar** güzel (*as* beautiful *as* you)

things to do

1.1 You go into a bank to change some money.

Clerk:	İyi günler. Ne arzu ediyorsunuz?
You:	[Say you want to change some English pound into Turkish lira.]
Clerk:	Ne kadar bozduracaksınız?
You:	[Say £100. Ask what the exchange rate is today.]
Clerk:	2400 Türk lirası, efendim. Lütfen, isminiz, adresiniz ve pasaport numaranız. Şurayı imzalayınız. … İşte paralarınız, efendim.
You:	[Say thank you.]

1.2 Unfortunately you have lost your handbag and report it to the police who need a list of what was in it. Can you give them a list in Turkish (using **benim** + the correct possessive endings)?

AT THE POST OFFICE

If you need to post a letter or card, it is advisable to go to the post office, as post boxes are quite scarce and not easy to recognise. Post offices are open from 8 am to midnight.

Postahane de bir konuşma/ Conversation at a post-office

Jill goes to the post-office to buy stamps and to post a parcel.

Posta memuru:	Buyurunuz, Hanımefendi!
Jill:	**İngiltere'ye bir kartpostal pulu kaç liradır?**
Posta memuru:	350 lira.
Daniel:	Ve **bir mektup pulu kaç lira?**
Posta memuru:	İngiltere'ye bir mektup pulu 500 liradır.
Jill:	Peki, **bize** altı tane 350 liralık ve on tane 500 liralık pul **veriniz.**
Posta memuru:	İşte pullar. Hepsi 7,100 lira tutar.
Daniel:	Ah, ve **biz** bu paketi acele Londra'ya **göndermeliyiz. Ne yapmalıyız?**
Posta memuru:	En çabuk özel ulak ile gider, lütfen şu fişi doldurunuz.
Jill:	Gönderen, adı, soyadı ve adresi. Alıcı, adı soyadı ve adresi.
Posta memuru:	Tamam mı! Evet tartmamız gerek. 16,000 liralık pul lazım. Lütfen şu beyan formunuda doldurunuz.
Daniel:	Peki, içeriği, fiyatı, hediye, şahsi eşya.

Buying stamps

postahane	post-office
posta memuru	post-office clerk
İngiltere'ye bir kartpostal pulu kaç liradır?	How much is a stamp for a postcard to England?
bir mektup	letter
bir taahhütlü mektup	registered letter
bir paket	parcel
Lütfen bize ... veriniz	Please give us ...
altı tane 350 liralık pul	6 × 350lira stamps
iki tane İngiltere pulu	2 stamps for England
Hepsi ... tutar	altogether, it comes to ...
ve biz ... göndermeliyiz	and we must send ...
bu paketi	this parcel
acele Birmingham'a	at once to Birmingham
Ne yapmalıyız?	What do we have to do?
En çabuk özel-ulak ile gider	Express delivery is the quickest way
Lütfen şu fişi doldurunuz	Please fill in this form
gönderen	sender
alıcı	recipient
ad, soyadı	name, surname
adres	address
Tamam mu?	Is that OK?
Tartmamız gerek	We must weigh it
16,000 liralık pul lazım	It needs 16,000 lira worth of stamps
şu beyan formunuda doldurunuz	fill in this declaration form too
içeriği	its contents
fiyatı	its price
hediye	present
şahsi esya	personal belongings
Posta kutusu nederedir?	Where is the post-box?

SPECIMEN ONLY

USING THE TELEPHONE

There are international telephone facilities both inside and outside post-offices.

Telefon kulübesinde/At the telephone kiosk

Jill:	Affedersiniz, **biz** buradan Birmingham'a **telefon edebilir miyiz?**
Posta memuru:	Kolaylıkla, yalnız çok bozuk para gerekiyor. Önce 99 (uluslararası kod) sonra 44 (İngiltere kodu) ve sonra da şehir kodu ve ev numarasını çeviriniz.
Daniel:	Çok teşekkürler, hoşça kalınız.
Posta memuru:	Bir şey değil. İyi tatiller.

Making a phone call

Buradan ... telefon edebilir miyiz?	Can we telephone from here
... Birmingham'a	... to Birmingham?
kolaylıkla	easily
Çok bozuk para gerekiyor	a lot of coins are needed
önce	firstly
sonra	later
uluslararası kod	international code
İngiltere kodu	code for England
şehir kodu	city code
ev numaranız	your house number
Lütfen çeviriniz ...	Please dial ...
Ben Londra'ya bir telgraf göndermek istiyorum	I want to send a telegram to London
Lütfen şu numaraya telefon etmem için yardım ediniz	Please help me phone this number

the way it works

... to England

If you want to say 'to England' you say **İngiltere'ye**. Look at the following phrases from the dialogue:

İngiltere'ye bir mektup pulu 500 liradır

It costs 500 lira for a letter *to England*

Biz bu paketi **Londra'ya** göndermeliyiz

We must send this parcel *to London*

These are examples of the *dative case* which in Turkish is used to mean *to*. Here is the full pattern of suffixes, in accordance with the vowel harmony rule:

last vowel of word	suffix
a, ı, o, u	-(y)a
e, i, ö, ü	-(y)e

... from Ankara

If you want to say 'from Ankara' you say **Ankara'dan**. This is an example of the *ablative case* which in Turkish is used to mean *from*. Here is the full pattern of suffixes, in accordance with the vowel harmony rule:

last vowel of word	suffix
a, ı, o, u	-dan
e, i, ö, ü	-den

However, after words ending in **ç, f, h, k, m p, x, t** you use –**tan/–ten**.

Pronouns

As well as the subject pronouns **ben**, **sen**, **o**, **biz**, **siz** and **onlar** we have met the indirect object pronouns **bana** (to me), **ona** (to him, her, it), **bize** (to us), **size** (to you) and **onlara** (to them) and the possessive pronouns **benim** (my), **onun** (him, her, it), **bizim** (our), **sizin** (your) and **onların** (their).

It is worth mentioning here the direct object pronouns. These are: **beni** (me), **onu** (him, her it), **bizi** (us), **sizi** (you) and **onları** (them).

How to say 'I must'

Bu paketi Londra'ya gönder**meliyiz**   We *must* send this parcel to London

To express duty, necessity or compulsion, insert the suffix **-meli/-malı** between the stem of the verb and its ending.

There are other ways of expressing need and obligation which it is useful to recognise and which we have seen in the dialogues:

gerek: Tartmamız **gerek** (it is necessary for us to weigh it)
gerekiyor: Çok bozuk para **gerekiyor** (it requires a lot of coins)
lazım: 16,000 liralık pul **lazım** (it needs 16,000 lira-worth of stamps)

things to do

4.3 You have gone to the post-office to buy some stamps.

Clerk: Buyurunuz, Hanımefendi.
You: [Greet him and ask for two stamps for postcards to England.]
Clerk: İşte pullar.
You: [Thank him and ask to be given four stamps for letters to the U.S.A.]
Clerk: Hepsi bu kadar mı?
You: [Say yes that's all and ask how much it comes to.]
Clerk: Hepsi 2,700 lira tutar.
You: [Say here is the money and ask if you can make a phone-call to London.]
Clerk: Evet, Hanımefendi. önce 99, sonra 44 (İngiltere kodu) çeviriniz, ve sonra şehir telefon numarasını çeviriniz.
You: [Thank him very much and say goodbye.]

4.4 There are a lot of things which you must do today. Can you tell your Turkish friend what they are?

1 buy some stamps

2 send a parcel to Australia

3 go to the bank

4 change some traveller's cheques

5 go to the coach station

6 buy a ticket to Izmir.

HIRING A CAR

efes
RENT A CAR
KiRALIK OTO tel, 14468

As Turkey is such a vast country with beautiful mountain ranges, driving is a good way of seeing it if you have the time. Most of the main roads linking the major cities are good but they get very busy with long-distance lorries and intercity coaches.

Car hire is expensive and prices vary from city to city. Turkish firms are cheaper than the usual European companies such as Avis, Budget, Hertz, etc.

Accidents and repairs: If you are involved in an accident, you must inform the police. An official report is necessary for any legal claims, insurance, etc. Most repair garages are very good and are usually situated on the outskirts of towns and cities.

Kiralık oto ofisinde/At the car-hire office

Jill and Daniel have some free time in the morning. Daniel hires a car to take Jill into the Anatolian plateau.

Daniel;   İyi sabahlar. **Bir araba kiralamak istiyorum.**

Ofis yetkilisi:	Hay hay efendim. Kaç kişi için? Küçük bir Peugeot ve büyük bir Ford Granada var. Ford Granada da radyo ve kaset çalar da var.
Jill:	Fiyatı nasıl oluyor? Günlük veya kilometre başına mı?
Ofis yetkilisi:	Gün başına.
Daniel:	Peki Ford'un fiyatı nedir?
Ofis yetkilisi:	İşte fiyat listesi ve sigorta ücreti.
Jill:	Biz Peugeot'u istiyoruz bir gün için.
Ofis yetkilisi:	Lütfen bana İngiliz ve uluslararası sürücü ehliyetinizi veriniz. Evet, her şey tamam. İşte arabanın anahtarı. Lütfen benim ile geliniz, arabayı görünüz.

Hiring a car

kiralık oto ofisi	Car hire office
Bir araba kiralamak istiyorum	I want to hire a car
Hay hay	Of course
Kaç kişi için?	For how many people?
Küçük bir Peugeot ve büyük bir Ford Granada	There is a small Peugeot and a big Ford Granada
Ford Granada da radyo ve kaset çalar da var	The Ford Granada has a radio csssette player
Fiyatı nasıl oluyor?	How is the price calculated?
Günlük veya kilometre başına mı?	Do we pay per day or kilometre?
gün başına	per day
Ford'un fiyatı nedir?	How much is the Ford?
İşte fiyat listesi ve sigorta ücretleri	Here is the price list and insurance cost
Lütfen bana İngiliz ve uluslararası sürücü ehliyetlerinizi veriniz	Please give me your English and international driving licences
Her şey tamam	Everything is in order
İşte arabanın anahtarı	Here is the key
Lütfen benim ile geliniz ve arabayı görünüz	Come with me and see the car
Depozite ödemeli miyim?	Do I have to pay a deposit?
Arabayı Konya'da teslim edebilir miyim?	Can I leave the car in Konya?

Other useful words and phrases

motorsiklet	motor bike	**karavan**	caravan
bisiklet	bicycle	**trafik**	traffic
uzun araç/TIR kamyonu	lorry	**trafik polisi**	traffic police

Petrol stations usually provide eating and toilet facilities. Garages are not generally self-service, and sometimes young people attend the car to clean the windscreen. A small tip (**bahşşiş**) is usually given out of courtesy.

In general, repair shops or garages are also attached to filling stations.

Benzincide/At the petrol station

Benzinci: Buyurunuz, efendim.
Daniel: **Benzin istiyoruz.** Süper benzininiz var mı?
Benzinci: Evet, ne kadar istiyorsunuz?
Daniel: **Lütfen 25 litrelik veriniz.** Lütfen yağ, su ve lastiklerin havasına bir bakınız.
Benzinci: Tamam efendim. 15,000 lira.
Daniel: Buyurunuz. Teşekkürler.

Buying petrol

benzin istiyoruz	We want some petrol
Süper benzininiz var mı?	Do you have super petrol?
Ne kadar istiyorsunuz?	How much do you want?
Lütfen 25 litrelik benzin veriniz	Please give me 25 litres of petrol
25,000 liralık normal benzin	25,000 lira's worth of normal petrol
Lütfen yağ/su/ve lastiklerin havasına bir bakınız	Please check the oil/water/and tyre pressure
Tamir yapıyor musunuz?	Do you do repairs?
Lütfen lastiklere biraz hava basınız	Please put some air into the tyres
Buraya park edebilir miyim?	Can I park here?
oto park	car park
Burada park yapmak yasaktır	Parking is prohibited here

A BREAKDOWN

Araba çalışmıyor!/The car won't start!

On their journey, they stop to rest at a picnic area. When they return to their car, it won't start. After checking the basics they decide to get a mechanic from a local garage and they walk to a nearby village.

Daniel:	Merhaba, bir araba ustası arıyoruz.
Köylü:	Merhaba. Şu köşede Tarık Usta var.
Jill:	Teşekkürler.
Tarık Usta:	Buyurunuz, ne istediniz?
Daniel:	**Arabamız** az ileride yolda **bozuldu**. Bir bakar mısınız?
Tarık Usta:	Hay hay, benim arabam ile gidelim.
Tarık Usta:	Sizin marş motoru bozuk. değiştirmek gerekiyor.
Daniel:	Peki, **onarabilir misiniz?**
Tarık Usta:	Evet, yedek parçamız var, fakat 45,000 liradır.
Daniel:	Peki, lütfen tamir ediniz, işte parası, yalnız bize fatura veriniz.

Problems with the car
(for parts of the car see page 84)

Bir araba ustası arıyoruz	We are looking for a mechanic
Şu köşede ... var	At that corner; there is ...
Tarık Usta	Master Tarık (**Usta** – a person with sound experience)
Ne istediniz?	What did you want?
Arabamız ... bozuldu	Our car has broken down
az ileride yolda	on the road, a little away from here
Bir bakar mısınız?	Will you take a look?
Hay hay, benim arabam ile gidelim	O.K., let's go in my car

Sizin marş motoru bozuk	Your starter motor is faulty
Değiştirmek gerekiyor	It is necessary to change it
Onarabilir misiniz?	Can you mend it?
Yedek parçamız var	We've got the spare part
tamir ediniz	please repair (it)
fakat/yalnız	but/only
Bize bir fatura veriniz	Please give us a receipt

Other useful phrases

Benzinimiz tükendi	We have run out of petrol
Bir tekerlek patlak	One of the tyres has a puncture
Araba niçin çalışmıyor?	Why is the car not working?
Bilmiyorum	I don't know
motor/su/yağ/akü-yü kontrol etmeliyim	I must check the engine/water/oil/battery
yağ pompası	the oil pump
vites kutusu	the gearbox
gaz kablosu	The accelerator cable
kayış	the fan-belt
... kırık	... is broken
... kopuk	... has broken apart
... çalışmıyor	... does not work

the way it works

Infinitive as subject

Look at the following phrase from the dialogue:
Değiştirmek gerekiyor   It is necessary to change.

As in English the infinitive can be used as a subject of the verb. Here are some other examples:

İzmir'den **gitmek** kolaydır	It is easy to go from Izmir
Telefon **etmek** kolaydır	It is easy to telephone

Simple past tense

Arabamız bozul**du**   Our car *has broken down* (**bozulmak** – to break down)

This is an example of the past tense. This tense is formed by inserting the suffix **-di-** (or **dı**, **du**, **dü** according to the vowel harmony rule) between the stem and the ending of the verb. This suffix becomes **-tı-/-tu-** (or **-ti/-tü**) after an unvoiced consonant.

Here are some further examples:

Ben yapt**ım**	I did (**yapmak** – to do)
Bir araba kirala**dık**	We hired a car (**kiralamak** – to hire)
İzmir'den git**ti**	He went from Izmir (**gitmek** – to go)
Ne iste**diniz?**	What did you want? (**istemek** –to want)

things to do

5.1 You are hiring a car.
   1 Say you would like a small car.
   2 Ask how much it costs for three days.
   3 Ask if you have to pay a deposit.
   4 Say you'll take the Peugeot and ask for the key.
   5 Ask if you can leave the car in Antalya.

5.2 You are at the petrol station.
   1 Ask for 30 litres of super petrol.
   2 Ask the attendant to check the tyre pressures.
   3 Ask if they do repairs.
   4 Say you want to buy a fan-belt.
   5 Ask for a receipt.

5.3 What do the following signs mean:

5.4 Your car has broken down. Can you:
   1 Ask someone where there is a garage.
   2 Tell the mechanic you have broken down.
   3 Say you have run out of petrol.
   4 Ask if the mechanic will come and look.

ACCIDENT AND EMERGENCY

Before travelling to Turkey, check whether you need any special inoculations. It is advisable to have a full health-insurance policy. If you use drugs on a regular basis it is advisable to take enough medication with you, although British prescriptions are valid. Most doctors speak English.

Nationals of countries with which Turkey has bilateral agreements are treated free of charge. Other foreign nationals have to pay small clinic fees at state hospitals (**hastahane**) and university hospitals. Some private and foreign hospitals are also available but their fees are usually very high. The Turkish medical profession is highly regarded, and doctors are well trained. You can get information about chemists' rotas (**nöbetci eczane**), by dialling 001. You can also get all basic items of healthcare, bodycare, cosmetics, toiletries, and basic drugs like aspirin, from the chemist's (**eczane**).

Bir kaza/An accident

While trying to reach the suitcase on top of the wardrobe, Daniel slips and falls off the chair. Jill is out, but the receptionist hears the noise.

Resepsiyoncu: Bu gürültü nedir? Ne oldu?
Daniel: **Yardım et**, sandalyeden düştüm.
                Korkarım ayak bileğimi incittim.
Resepsiyoncu: Eyvah, nasıl çok ağrıyor mu?
Daniel: Evet, **bir araba bul**. Polikliniğe
                gidelim.

An accident

Bu gürültü nedir?	What is this noise?
Ne oldu?	What has happened?
Yardım et	Help!
düştüm	I fell over
sandalyeden düştüm	I fell off the chair
Korkarım ...	I fear that ...
... ayak bileğim	... my ankle
nasıl çok ağrıyor mu?	Does it hurt very much?
Bir araba çağır/bul	Get a car
Polikliniğe gidelim	Let's go to the polyclinic

Bölge polikliniğinde/At the polyclinic

Doktor: Geçmiş olsun. Ne oldu?

Daniel: Düştüm ve sanırım ayak bileğimi incittim.

Doktor: Bir dakika, neresi ağrıyor?

Daniel: Evet, **tam orası çok ağrıyor.**

Doktor: Hemşire hanım, lütfen bir ayak bileği röntgeni çektiriniz, ve bir ağrı kesici iğne yapınız.

Daniel: Lütfen bana iğne yerine hap veriniz.

Hemşire: Peki.

Doktor: Üzülmeyiniz, kırık yok, yalnız burkulma var. Size şu reçeteyi veriyorum, bir eczaneden alınız. Geçmiş olsun.

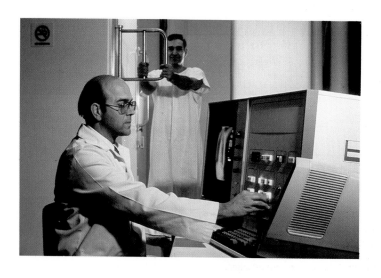

Diagnosis
(for parts of the body see page 83)

sanırım ...	I think that ...
Neresi ağrıyor?	Where does it hurt?
Tam orası çok ağrıyor	Right there it hurts badly
Hemşire hanım, ...	Nurse, ...
bir ayak bileği röntgeni çekiniz	take an X-ray of the ankle
Bir ağrı kesici iğne yapınız	give a pain-killing injection
iğne	injection
bana ... hap veriniz	give me a tablet
yerine	instead of
Üzülmeyiniz	Please don't worry
kırık yok	there is nothing broken
yalnız burkulma var	it is only twisted
Size şu reçeteyi veriyorum	I am giving you this prescription
Lütfen bir eczaneden alınız	Please get it from a chemist
Geçmiş olsun	May you make a fast recovery

Eczanede/At the chemist's

Eczacı: Buyurunuz, ne istiyorsunuz?
Jill: İyi günler, **şu ilaçlar sizde var mı?**
Eczacı: Bir dakika, evet hepsi var. Bu ağrı kesicidir. Günde üç defa alacaksınız ve bu da adele kremi, lütfen az olarak ağrıyan yere sürünüz.
Jill: Çok teşekkürler, işte paranız.

At the chemist's
(for a list of toiletries, etc., see page 81)

Şu ilaçlar sizde var mı?	Do you have these drugs?
ilaçlar	drugs
Hepsi var	Everything is here
Bu bir ağrı kesicidir	This is a pain-killer
Günde üç defa bir adet alacaksınız	Take one three times a day
... yemeklerden önce/sonra	... before/after meals
Bu bir adele kremi	This is a muscle cream
Lütfen ağrıyan yere sürünüz	Please apply it where it hurts

55

Other useful phrases

Yaralımısınız?	Are you hurt?
Ağrım var	I am in pain
Hastayım	I am ill
Röntgen filmi	X-ray
Bir doktor/dişçi/hastabakıcı/-ya gerek var	A doctor/dentist/nurse is needed
En yakın poliklinik nerededir?	Where is the nearest polyclinic?
En yakın eczane nerededir?	Where is the nearest chemist's?
Baş ağrısı için bir şeyiniz var mı?	Have you got something for a headache?
Boğazım ağrıyor	I have a sore throat
İshal oldum	I have diarrhoea
İshal için bir şeyiniz var mı?	Have you got something for diarrhoea?
Günde kaç tane almalıyım?	How many do I have to take per day?
Kaç defa almalıyım?	How many times do I have to take?
... üç defa	... three times
Midem de hazımsızlık var	I have indigestion
Saman nezlesi olurum	I have hay-fever
Nefes ala mıyorum	I can't breathe
uyuyamıyorum	sleep
Midem bulandı	I've been sick
Midem ağrıyor	I have stomach-ache
Başım ...	a headache
Kulağım ...	ear-ache
Dişim ...	tooth-ache
Sırtım ...	back-ache
Gözümde bir şey var	I've got something in my eye
elimi/kolumu yaktım	I have burnt my hand/arm
Benim ... ağrıyor	My ... hurts
Benim bileğim şişti/ kırıldı/incindi	My wrist is swollen/ broken/sprained
Sıcak/soğuk hissediyorum	I feel hot/cold
Güneşte yandım	I have sunburn
Ben diyabetiğim/astımlıyım	I am diabetic/asthmatic
Ben hamileyim	I am pregnant
Ben doğum kontrol hapı alıyorum	I am on the pill
Penisiline karşı alerjim var	I'm allergic to penicillin

Other emergencies

If you are in trouble, go to the nearest police station (**Karakol**), the embassy (**Elçilik**), or ask for help at the hotel.

Karakol nerededir?	Where is the police station?
Acil hastahanesi nerededir?	Where is the emergency hospital?
Bir kaza oldu	There has been an accident
Polis çağırınız	Call the police
sigorta şirketi	insurance company
Sizin hatanızdı	It was your fault

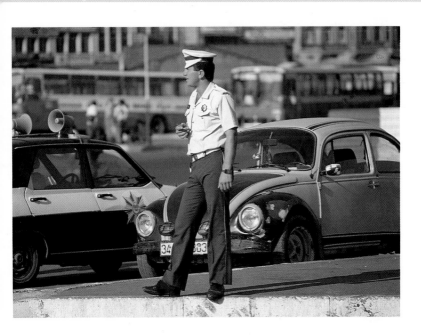

Disaster! (Acil durumlar!)

İmdat! or Yardım!	Help!
Polis!	Police!
Acil Hastahanesi	Emergency Hospital
trafik Hastahanesi	Traffic Accident Hospital
doğum hastahanesi	Maternity Hospital
İlk Yardım/Ambülans	First Aid/Ambulance
Tehlike	Danger
Yangın var	Fire
Dikkat	Caution
Yüzme simidi	Lifejacket
Yangın sondürücü	Fire extinguisher
İtfaiye	Fire brigade

Loss and Theft

Biletimi kaybettim	I've lost my ticket
Anahtarımı ...	my key
Fotoğraf makinemi ...	my camera
Pasaportumu ...	my passport
Çek kartımı ...	my cheque card
Biletim çalındı	My ticket was stolen
Radyom ...	My radio ...
El çantam ...	My handbag ...
Kayboldum	I am lost
Kayıp eşya ofisi	Lost property office

57

things to do

5.5 You have an upset stomach and you go to the chemist for advice.

Chemist:	Yardım edebilir miyim?
You:	[Ask her if she has something for diarrhoea.]
Chemist:	Bu haplar çok iyidir.
You:	[Say OK you'll have them and ask how many a day you should take.]
Chemist:	Günde dört defa ikişer hap.
You:	[Say thank you and ask how much they are.]

5.6 **Neresi ağrıyor?** Various guests at your hotel are suffering from a number of ailments. Can you explain to the doctor what is wrong with each of them?

Kate:	David:	Peter:	Maggie:
sunburn	stomach-ache	sprained ankle	burnt arm

and finally, can you explain what happened to you? You fell over on the beach and injured your knee.

5.7 Here are some of the things that you and your family have mislaid. Can you tell the police what each of them is in Turkish? Use . . . **kaybettim**.

Sabahleyin

SPORT AND LEISURE

In the coastal areas, facilities for sea sports and activities may include fishing, sailing and windsurfing, scuba-diving, water-skiing and water football. In the mountains you will find many resorts for mountaineering, skiing and hunting. There are few restrictions on sports like fishing and hunting but it is advisable to check with the local information office beforehand.

Hangi sporları yaparsınız/
What sports do you play?

Daniel's ankle is much better and he and Jill have challenged each other to a game of tennis on the hotel tennis court.

Cüneyt:	Buyurunuz Bay Daffin, ne istiyorsunuz?
Daniel:	iyi günler Cüneyt Bey, biz bu öğleden sonra tenis oynamak istiyoruz. Tenis sahası boş mu acaba?
Cüneyt:	Bir dakika. Evet işte listemiz, **saat kaç için**?
Daniel:	Saat dört gibi, olabilir mi?
Cüneyt:	Şanslısınız, boş, efendim. Lütfen dörde beş kala gelip sahanın anahtarını benden alınız.
Jill:	Çok teşekkürler.

Making arrangements

bu öğleden sonra	in the afternoon
Biz ... tenis oynamak istiyoruz	We want to play tennis
Tenis sahası boş mu acaba?	We wonder if the tennis court is available?
İşte listemiz	Here is our list
Saat kaç için?	At what time?
Saat dört gibi, olabilir mi?	Can it be about four o'clock?
Şanslısınız	You are lucky
dörde beş kala gelip	about five to four
sahanın anahtarını benden alınız	come to get the key of the court from me

Other useful phrases

Ben sporu severim	I like sport
Ben futbol oynamasını severim	I like playing football
golf	golf
tenis	tennis
basketbol	basketball
masa topu	table-tennis
Ben yüzmeyi severim	I like swimming
koşmayı	jogging
ata binmeyi	horse-riding
yelkenciliği	sailing
kayak yapmayı	skiing
su kayağı yapmayı	water-skiing
yürümeyi	walking
Ben spor seyretmesini severim	I like watching sports

Ben futbol seyretmesini severim	I like watching football
Bir stadyum var	There is a stadium
Stadyum nerededir?	Where is the stadium?
Basketbol sahası	Basketball hall
voleybol sahası	volleyball hall
tenis sahası	tennis court
yüzme havuzu	swimming pool
Bir tenis raketi istiyorum	I want a tennis racket
bir tenis topu	a tennis ball

the way it works

Word coupling

If you want to use two nouns together, the case endings depend on whether the relationship between them is **(a)** merely descriptive (*tennis court*) or **(b)** grammatically linked (*the keys to the court*) where the first noun actually belongs to the second.

a) The first noun is in its nominative form (i.e. with no ending) and the second takes the *accusative* case ending (see Tuesday, page 24).

Examples of this construction include:

dolmuş durağ**ı**   dolmus stop
çay bardağ**ı**   tea cup
and in this unit:
tenis saha**sı**   tennis court

b) The first noun appears with a *genitive* suffix (see Thursday, page 39) and the second takes the accusative ending.

Examples of this construction include:

bavul**un** anahtar**ı**   the keys of the suitcase
                    (lit. of the suitcase the keys)
ev**in** merdivenler**i**   the stairs of the house
                    (lit. of the house the stairs)
palto**nun** düğme**si**   the button of the coat
                    (lit. of the coat the button)
and in this unit:
tenis saha**sının** anahtar**ı**   the keys of the tennis court
                    (lit. of the court the keys)

Compare this construction with the possessive on page 40.

Exclamations

Here is a list of some of the words used to express emotion, wishes or simply to attract someone's attention.

A, hah!	I say! Oh! Ha!
Ay!	Oh!
Aman!	What a shame! Oh dear!
Haydi!	Come on!
Of!	Ugh!
Ya!	Is that so? Really?
Ne!	What?
Hey!	Hey, There!
Yahu!	I say (reproachfully)
Yazık!/Vah vah!	What a pity!
Allah Allah!	Good heavens!
Maşallah!	Wonderful!
İnşallah!	God willing!
Aferin!	Well done!
Hay hay!	Certainly, by all means!

Sabahleyin

things to do

6.1 Can you say whether you like the following sports?
Use either **Ben ... severim** (I like), **Ben ... oynamasını severim**
(I like playing) or **Ben ... seyretmesini severim** (I like watching):

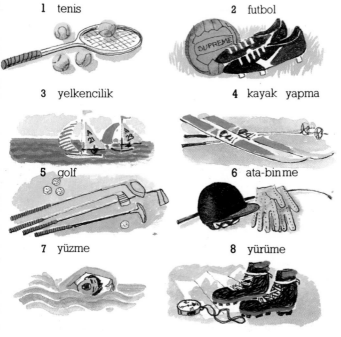

1 tenis

2 futbol

3 yelkencilik

4 kayak yapma

5 golf

6 ata-binme

7 yüzme

8 yürüme

6.2 You want to play tennis and you have arrived at a sports centre
with a friend.

You: [Say you want to play tennis and ask the person in
              charge if there is a tennis court available.]

Attendant: Bir dakika. Saat kaç için oynamak istiyorsunuz?

You: [Say this morning at about eleven.]

Attendant: Şanslısınız, boş, efendim. Lütfen, sahanın ahahtarını
              benden alınız.

You: [Say that's fine. Say you'd like to hire some tennis
              balls.]

6.3 Can you ask where to go to watch the following sports events:
1 football match
2 swimming gala
3 water-skiing competition
4 basketball tournament.

ENTERTAINMENT

Bir açık hava eğlencesi/
An open-air entertainment

Jill and Daniel have been given free tickets to an open-air concert in the town centre for the evening.

Cem: Haydi **çabuk olunuz!** Konser saat yirmi birde başlayacak.
Jill: Peki, **işte hazırım.**
Daniel: Bir dakika! Ceketimi almalıyım.
They enter the open-air concert area.
Jill: Aman Allah! Çok kalabalık.
Daniel: Programda neler var?
Cem: Konser Türk halk müziği ile başlayacak. Sonra Türk sanat müziğinden şarkılar var. Daha sonra, Türk hafif müziğinden örnekler sunulacak.
Jill: Folklör ekibi var mı?
Cem: Evet, onlar da Türk oyunları sunacaklar.
Daniel: Değişik çalgı aletleri var. Bize adlarını söyler misin?
Cem: Pekala. Saz, davul, zurna halk müziğinde kullanılır. Ud, çümbüş, tambur, saz, keman ve kanun, darbuka sanat müziğinde görülür. Hafif müzikte gitar, elektronik piyano, davullar vardır.
Jill: Susalım program başlıyor . . .

Listening to music

çabuk olunuz	Hurry up/Be quick
Konser saat yirmi birde başlayacak	The concert is going to start at twenty-one hours
İşte hazırım	Here, I am ready
Ceketimi almalıyım!	I must take my jacket!
Çok kalabalık	It's very crowded
Programda neler var?	What is there on the programme?
Konser ... başlayacak	The concert will begin ...
... Türk halk müziği ile ...	... with Turkish folk music
sonra/daha sonra	afterwards/after that
şarkı/oyun	song/dance
Türk sanat müziğinden şarkılar var	There are songs from Turkish classical music
Türk hafif müziğinden örnekler	Examples of Turkish pop music
... sunulacak	... will be performed
Bir folklör ekibi var mı?	Is there a folk-group?
Onlar da Türk oyunları sunacaklar	They will also perform some Turkish dances
Değişik çok çalgı aletleri var	There are many kinds of instruments
Bize adlarını söyler misin?	Can you give us their names?
Saz, davul ve zurna ...	Lute, drum and flute ...
... folklör müziğinde kullanılır	... are used in folk-music
Ud, çümbüş, tambur,	Ud, ducimer, lute,
keman ve kanun, darbuka,	violin, zither, tom-tom,
gitar, elektronik piyano	guitar, electronic keyboard
... kullanılır	... is used
... görülür	... is seen
Susalım	Let's be quiet, hush!
program başlıyor	the programme is starting

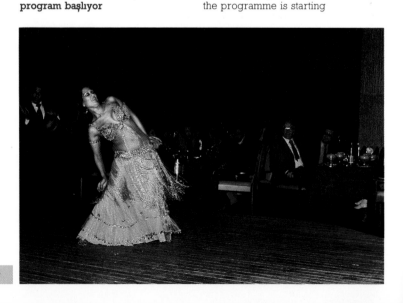

Yemekli bir gazinoda/Dinner at a casino

Later, Jill, Esra, Daniel and Cem are dining out at a Turkish taverna, where there is live music and belly-dancing.

Jill: Dansöz çok güzel dans ediyor.
Cem: Haydi biz de katılalım. . . .
Dansöz: Gel canım gel! Şöyle kalça atacağız. Tamam oluyor.
Jill: Böyle dans etsem, çok kilo kaybederim.
Cem: Aferin, çok güzel.

Esra: Nasıl hoşuna gittimi, ne düşünüyorsun?

Jill: Evet, hoşuma gitti. Kilo kaybetmek için iyi bir yöntem.

Let's dance!

dansöz	belly-dancer
Dansöz çok güzel dans ediyor	The belly-dancer is dancing very well
Haydi biz de katılalım!	Let's join in as well!
Gel canım gel!	Come here, my dear!
Şöyle kalça atacağız	We wiggle our hips like this
Tamam oluyor	That's fine
Böyle dans etsem, çok kilo kaybederim!	If I dance like this, I'll lose a lot of weight!
Aferin, çok güzel!	Well done, very good!
Nasıl hoşuna gittimi?	Did you like it?
Ne düşünüyorsun?	What do you think?
Kilo kaybetmek için güzel bir yöntem	It's a very good way of losing weight

the way it works

The passive

Look at these expressions from the first dialogue:

Saz, davul ve zurna ... **kullanılır**	Lute, drum and flute ... are used
keman darbuka ... **görülür**	violin and tom-tom ... are seen

These are examples of the Turkish passive, which is formed by adding **-il-** or **-ul-** to the verb stem, after all consonants except **l**.

sevmek (to love)	sev**il**mek (to be loved)
görmek (to see)	gör**ül**mek (to be seen)
kullanmak (to use)	kullan**ıl**mak (to be used)

Verbs which end in **-l** and/or a vowel have the passive suffix **-in-** or **-n-**:

almak (to take)	al**ın**mak (to be taken)
okumak (to read)	ok**un**mak (to be read)

Note: examples of the passive are also to be found in the dialogue in Unit 5, page 54: kırıldı = is broken, inc**in**di = is sprained, çal**ın**dı = is stolen.

Conditional sentences

Jill says these words in the second dialogue:

Ben böyle dans ed**erse**m, çok kilo kaybederim. If I dance like this I will lose a lot of weight

Here the verb is **dans etmek**. The suffix **-r-** indicates that it is in the aorist tense. The **-se-** suffix which follows indicates the conditional mode and the **-m** indicates the first person I.

Here is another example:

Akşam erken gel**irse**niz sinemaya gideriz If you come early tonight, we can go to the cinema

Lets ...!

This expression is formed by using the interjection **haydi** at the beginning of the action and the suffix **-(y)alim/-(y)elim** at the end of the verb. Here are some examples:

Haydi, lokantaya gid**elim**	Let's go to the restaurant
Haydi, (biz) katıl**alım**	Let's join in
Haydi, yüz**elim**	Let's swim
Haydi, bir kayık kirala**yalım**	Let's hire a boat

things to do

.4 Read the two advertisements below and answer the following questions, in Turkish. Each of the questions refer to both advertisements.

1 What is being advertised here?
2 What kind of music will be played?
3 What time does the performance begin?
4 How much are the tickets?

*Eşsiz bir
yemek ve müzik ziyafeti*
Fasl-ı Konak

*Geçmişin unutulmaz Fasıl gecelerini
bir Osmanlı vezirinin konağında yaşayın.
Musikimizin klasik, neo klasik en seçkin
eserlerini TRT sanatçıları Recep Birgit,
Galip Sokullu, Melihat Gülses, Tülay
Canik, Refi!. Akbulut ve Koray Safkan'dan
her hafta PAZARTESİ ve PERŞEMBE
geceleri dinleyerek nostaljiyi tadın.*

REŞAT PAŞA KONAĞI
RESTAURANT
Tel: 361 34 11-361 34 87-361 35 89

TALKING ABOUT YOURSELF

Meslekler/Occupations

Jill and Daniel are invited to a reception party given by their
Turkish friends Tarık and Neslihan.

Tarık:	(*to Jill*) Size arkadaşım Mehmet Akçapınarı tanıştırayım.
Mehmet:	Tanıştığımıza memnun oldum.
Tarık:	Daniel, eşim Neslihan ile tanıştınız sanıyorum.
Daniel:	Evet, Nasılsınız Neslihan Hanım?
Neslihan:	Teşekkürler. Jill Hanım siz nasılsınız?
Jill:	Teşekkürler, iyiyiz.
Neslihan:	İzniniz ile, diğer misafirler geliyorlar. Lütfen. kendi evinizde gibi hissediniz.
Mehmet:	(*to Daniel*) Affedersiniz, mesleğiniz nedir?
Daniel:	**Ben bir elektronik mühendisiyim.**
Tarık:	Çok iyi bir meslek. Modern yaşantıda elektronik çok şey kullanıyoruz.
Daniel:	Sizin mesleğiniz nedir?
Tarık:	Ben bir cerrahım. Eşim diş doktorudur.
Mehmet:	Ben de öğretmenim, bir okulun baş öğretmeniyim.
Tarık:	Jill Hanım, sizin mesleğiniz nedir?
Jill:	Ah, ben bir ev hanımıyım.
Mehmet:	Evet, sizin işiniz gerçekten çok yorucu! Ev işi, çoçuklar, yemek, sonra biz erkekler!

What do you do?

For a list of professions see page 84.

Size arkadaşım ... tanıştırayım	Let me introduce my friend to you
Tanıştığımıza memnun oldum	I am pleased to meet you
eşim ... ile tanıştınız	you have met my wife/husband ...
sanıyorum	I think
İzniniz ile ...	With your permission ...

Diğer misafirler geliyorlar	Other guests are coming
Kendi evinizde gibi hissediniz	Please feel at home
Sizin mesleğiniz nedir?	What is your occupation?
Ben bir mühendisim	I am an engineer
(Ben) koleje gidiyorum	I go to college
Bir fabrikada çalışıyorum	I work in a factory
Bir bankada ...	in a bank
Bir hastahanede ...	at a hospital
İşsizim	I am unemployed
Sizin işiniz gerçekten zor	Your work is certainly hard
çok iyi bir meslek	a very good occupation
modern yaşantıda ...	in modern life ...
elektronik çok şey kullanıyoruz	we use a lot of electronic things

cerrah	surgeon
eşim diş doktorudur	my wife is a dentist (*lit.* dental doctor)
Ev işi, çoçuklar, yemek,	housework, children, food,
sonra biz erkekler!	then us men!

THE WEATHER

Hava durumu/Weather conditions

Daniel: **Bugün** hava gerçekten **çok sıcak**.

Mehmet: Evet, özellikle bu ay genel olarak hava sıcaktır.

Tarık: İngiltere'de hava nasıldır?

Jill: Genellikle yağmurlu ve kapalıdır.

Mehmet: İngiltere'de çok sis var. Hava nemlidir, doğru mu?

Daniel: Evet. Türkiye'de kışın soğuk olur mu?

Neslihan: Evet. Ege ve Akdeniz kıyıları dışında kış soğuktur. Fakat Türkiye'de dört mevsim yaşanır.

Jill: **Ben** sıcağı **tercih ederim**. Soğuk ve karlı havadan hoşlanman.

Daniel: Ben rüzgarlı havayı sevmem.

Mehmet: Biz de güneşli ve açık, sıcak ve kuru havayı severiz.

What's the weather like?

Bugün çok sıcak	It is very hot today
gerçekten	in fact
özellikle	especially
genellikle/genel onlarak	in general
Hava nasıl?	What is the weather like?
Hava sıcak/soğuk	It is hot/cold
güneşli/açık	sunny/clear
rüzgarlı/bulutlu, kapalı	windy/cloudy
yağmurlu/karlı	rainy/snowy
sisli/puslu	foggy
nemli/kuru	damp/dry
Yağmur yağıyor	It is raining
Kar yağıyor	It is snowing
Rüzgar esiyor	The wind is blowing
Fırtına çıkıyor	The storm is coming
kışın soğuk olur mu?	Is it cold in winter?
Ege ve Akdeniz kıyıları dışında	Apart from the Aegean and Meditteranean coasts
Fakat Türkiye'de dört mevsim yaşanır	But in Turkey four seasons are lived
Ben ... tercih ederim	I prefer
Ben ... sevmem/hoşlanmam	I don't like

the way it works

How to say what you do

Ben bir mühendis**im**	I'm an engineer
doktor**um**	a doctor
müdür**üm**	a manager

This construction uses the verb **imek** (to be). It is a [noun + (imek)] structure.

But certain occupational words are made up from two or more nouns coupled together (e.g. electronics engineer). When this happens, you add a coupling suffix (elektronik mühendisi + im), which therefore needs a **y** as a liaison letter.
Ben bir banka müdürüy**üm** I'm a bank manager

Two of these compound structures appeared in the dialogue:
Ben bir elektronik mühendisiy**im** I'm an electronics engineer
Ben bir ev hanımıy**ım** I'm a housewife

... and where you work

To say where you work use the locative case:

Ben bir fabrika**da** bir mühendisim	I'm an engineer in a factory
Ben bir çocuk hastahanesin**de** doktorum	I'm a doctor in a children's hospital

Talking about the weather

Hava nasıl? What's the weather like?
The answer may be constructed as follows:
Hava sıcaktır It's hot

The **(tir/dir)** part which means *is* (see Monday, page 5) can be omitted in conversation.

If you want to ask for a weather forecast, you need to use the simple future tense;
Hava nasıl **olacak?** What will the weather be like?
Hava soğuk **olacak** It will be cold

To say 'it is raining' one uses the present tense of **yağmak** + noun **yağmur** (*rain*).
yağmur **yağıyor**   it is raining
kar **yağıyor**   it is snowing

To say 'it will rain' use the same construction with the future tense of **yağmak**.
yağmur **yağacak**   it will rain
kar **yağacak**   it will snow

things to do

.1 Everyone in your party is talking about what they do. Can you join in?

Mark: an architect   Susan: an accountant

Charles: a businessman

Anna: a taxi driver   Bernard: a dustman   Helen: an artist

What do *you* do for a living?

7.2

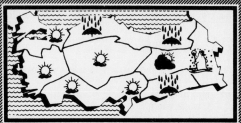

| AÇIK | KARLI | KAPALI | YAĞMUR | SİSLİ |

İSTANBUL: Parçalı az bulutlu, -2°/6°
ANKARA: Parçalı bulutlu, -8°/4°
İZMİR: Az bulutlu, açık, -1°/11°
ADANA: Az bulutlu, açık, 7°/18°
ANTALYA: Az bulutlu, açık, 6°/16°
EDİRNE: Parçalı az bulutlu, -4°/9°
ESKİŞEHİR: Parçalı bulutlu, -8°/3°
İZMİT: Parçalı az bulutlu, -2°/8°
SAKARYA: Parçalı az bulutlu, -2°/8°
ZONGULDAK: Çok bulutlu, yağmurlu -9°/3°

AVRUPA'DA ÖNEMLİ MERKEZLER

LONDRA: Parçalı bulutlu, 8°
PARİS: Az bulutlu, 7°
ZÜRİH: Az bulutlu, 6°
CENEVRE: Az bulutlu, 15°
ROMA: Parçalı bulutlu, 14°
ATİNA: Az bulutlu, 14°

1 What's the weather like in İstanbul?
2 Is it raining in İzmir?
3 Is it snowing in the mountains?
4 Is it windy on the south coast?

TALKING ABOUT YOUR STAY

Görüşleriniz/Your observations

Daniel and Jill are talking to a Turkish tourist guide, Nermin.

Jill:	Biz burada kısa bir tatildeyiz.
Nermin:	Kaç gün kalacaksınız?
Daniel:	İki hafta.
Nermin:	Daha önceden Türkiye'ye geldiniz mi?
Jill:	Hayır, bu bizim ilk gelişimiz.
Nermin:	Nerede kalıyorsunuz?
Daniel:	Yusuf Otel'de kalıyoruz.
Nermin:	Buradan hoşlandınız mı?
Jill:	Evet, bize göre Türkiye çok değişik ve ilginç bir ülke.
Daniel:	Bizce, Türkler çok konuksever insanlar. Türkiye'nin çok zengin bir tarihi ve kültürü var.

Have you enjoyed your stay?

Biz burada ...	We are here ...
... kısa bir tatildeyiz	... for a short holiday
... bir iş ziyaretinde	... on a business trip
... eski camileri incelemekte	... to study the old mosques
Kaç gün kalacaksınız?	How many days are you staying?
iki hafta/ay/yaklaşık iki gün	two weeks/months/about two days
Daha önceden Türkiye'ye geldiniz mi?	Have you been to Turkey before?
Mayıs ayının sonundan beri ...	... since the end of May
... buradayım	I've been here ...
bu bizim ilk gelişimiz	this is our first visit
Nerede kalıyorsunuz?	Where are you staying?
Yusuf Otel'de kalıyoruz	We are staying at the Hotel Yusuf
Buradan hoşlandınız mı?	Have you enjoyed (lit. liked) it here?
Bize göre .../Bana göre ...	In our view ....In my view ...
... çok değişik ve ilginç	... very different and interesting
Türkler çok konuksever insanlar	Turks are very hospitable people
Türkiye'nin çok zengin bir tarihi ve kültürü var	Turkey has a very rich history and culture

TALKING ABOUT HOBBIES

Hobileriniz nelerdir?/What are your hobbies?

Cem, Esra, Jill and Daniel are talking about their hobbies.

Cem: Ben açık hava sporlarını severim. Her hafta sonunda, bisikletle yakın köylere giderim. Pazartesi günleri golf oynarım. Cumartesi öğleden sonra atçılık kulübüne giderim.

Jill: Ben klasik müziği çok severim. Piyano ve kemanı iyi çalarım. Haftada bir defa konsere giderim. Salı günleri keman, cuma günleride piyano dersleri alırım.

Esra: Ben biraz sanatkarım. Resim çizerim ve sulu boya yaparım. Çarşamba akşamları çömlekçilik kursuna giderim. Şehirde bütün sergilere giderim.

Daniel: Ben macerayı severim. Dağcılık ve kayak yaparım. Yazın denizde dalgıçlık yaparım. Haftada iki günde uçuş okuluna giderim.

Sports and hobbies
For a list of sporting activities see page 84.

... severim	I like ...
Ben açık hava sporlarını severim	I like open-air sports
Hafta sonunda	At the weekend
Her hafta sonunda	At weekends

bisikletle	by bicycle
yakın köylere	to nearby villages
her Pazartesi/Cumartesi	on Mondays/Saturdays
her Pazartesi sabahı/akşamı	on Monday mornings/evenings
golf oynarım	I play golf
golf kulübü/atcılık kulübü	golf-club/riding-club
Ben piyano çalarım	I play (the) piano
keman/saz	violin/lute
günde bir defa	once a day
haftada iki defa	twice a week
Konsere giderim	I go to a concert
piyano dersleri alırım	I take piano lessons
Ben biraz sanatkarım	I am a bit of an artist
Resim çizerim	I draw
ve sulu boya/yağlı boya yaparım	and do water-colours/oil painting
çömlekçilik kursu	pottery course
bütün sergiler	all exhibitions
Ben macerayı severim	I like adventure
Dağcılık yaparım	I go mountaineering
kayak/dalgıçlık/uçuş	skiing/scuba-diving/flying

the way it works

How many times, how often

In order to express this concept, use **defa** or **kere** together with the number of occurrences or happenings.

bir **defa** or bir **kere**   once
iki **defa** or iki **kere**   twice
üç **defa** or üç **kere**   three times

If these are used with a period of time they may appear as such:
haftada bir **defa** or haftada bir **kere**:   once a week
yılda iki **defa**   or yılda iki **kere**:   twice a year

If the events take place regularly:
her pazartesi or pazartesi günleri: every Monday
her hafta: every week
her hafta salı günleri: every week on Tuesday
her hafta Salı günü akşamları: every week on Tuesday evenings

The aorist tense: a reminder

The aorist tense is frequently used in promises, in requests, in stage directions, in vivid present cases, and also in expressing a continuing activity or habit, as in this unit:

Ben piyano çala**rım**   I play (the) piano
Cumartesi atçılık kulübüne gide**rim**   On Saturdays I go to the riding-club

things to do

7.3 See if you can fill in this form giving details about yourself in Turkish:

```
Ad: ...........................................................................
Soyadı: .....................................................................
Doğum tarihi: ...........................................................
Doğum yeri: ..............................................................
Medeni Durum: .........................................................
Meslek: .....................................................................
İş yeri: ......................................................................
Hobiler: ....................................................................
Sevilen spor dalları: .................................................
Sevilen müzik: ..........................................................
Sevilen sanat dalları: ...............................................
Sevilen renkler: ........................................................
Sevilen ülkeler: ........................................................
```

.4 At their job interviews two people are asked about their hobbies.

    A You are Alison. Give the interviewer the following information:
1. You like classical music.
2. You play the violin and the piano.
3. You go to a concert about once a week.
4. On Monday evenings you go to a music club.

    B You are Colin. Give the interviewer the following information:
1. You are an artist.
2. You like drawing and doing water-colours.
3. You are doing a pottery course on Thursday mornings.
4. You go to all the exhibitions.

KEY TO EXERCISES

1.1 Merhaba Bay Oğuzkan. Hoşça Kalınız Bay Oğuzkan. 2 Merhaba Engin Bey. Hoşça Kalınız Engin Bey. 3 Merhaba Bayan Köylü. Hoşça Kalınız Bayan Köylü 4 Merhaba Bayan Yarımcı. Hoşça Kalınız Bayan Yarımcı.
1.2 1 Merhaba. Nasılsınız? 2 Günaydın. 3 İyi akşamlar. Tanıştığımıza memnun oldum. 4 İyi günler. Nasılsınız?
1.3 You: Merhaba, Oğuz Bey. You: Çok teşekkür ederim, iyiyim. Ya siz? You: Tanıştığımıza memnun oldum. Nasılsınız?
1.4 You: İyi sabahlar. Boş odanız var mı? You: Bir hafta için. You: Ben tek kişilik duşlu bir oda istiyorum. You: Peki. Odada duş var mı? You: Peki. Ücreti ne kadar?
1.5 Bira, kırmızı şarap, meyva suyu, maden suyu, çay.

2.1 Frances için, ekmek, beyaz peynir ve bir Türk kahvesi getiriniz. Peter için, ekmek, tereyağı ve reçel getiriniz lütfen. Andrew için, ekmek, zeytin ve meyva suyu getiriniz lütfen. Jane için, ekmek, reçel ve bir Türk kahvesi getiriniz.
2.2 1 Dört kişilik bir masanız var mı? 2 Lütfen listeyi getiriniz. 3 İçecek neler var? 4 Ben, bir, çorba, bir şiş kebap, bir Adana kebap ve bir karışık salata istiyorum. 5 Bir şişe rakı lütfen. 6 Hesabı getirir misiniz?
2.3 You: Lüften, bir kilo üzüm istiyorum. You: Şeftaliler kaç lira? You: Bir kilo istiyorum, lütfen You: Lüften, yarım kilo domates veriniz. You: Hayır. Hepsi bu kadar? Ne kadar?
2.4 200 gram white-curd cheese
a loaf of bread
1 litre of milk
1 packet of tea
½ kilo of rice
250 grams of olives.
2.5 1 Küçük mavi bir kilim [satın almak istiyorum] 2 Semaver 3 Büyük bir seramik tabak 4 Bir kaç tesbih taşı 5 Beyaz bir gömlek.

3.1 1 Affedersiniz, Postahane

nerededir? 2 Turist Enformasyon bürosu nerededir? 3 Osman Paşa Caddesi nerededir? 4 İstasyon (gar) nerededir?
3.2 1 Kaleye nasıl gidebiliriz? (gidebilirim) or Kaleye nasıl giderim. 2 Limana nasıl gidebilirim? 3 Müzeye nasıl gidebilirim? 4 Camiye nasıl gidebilirim?
3.3 1 Go straight along this road, then take the first street on the (turn) right. The mosque is there. 2 Go straight along this road. [Take] the first street on the left. The post office is there, on the corner. 3 Go straight along this road. The station is at the end of the road, on the right.
3.4 You: Hitit Müzesine gitmek istiyorum. Buradan oraya nasıl gidebilirim (or giderim)? You: Dolmuş durağı nerededir? You: Dolmuş bizi oraya dosdoğru götürecek mi? You: Çok teşekkürler.
3.5 (a) Efes'e İzmir'e/Bodrum'a/ Kuşadası'na otobüs ne zaman hareket ediyor? or Efes'e İzmir'e/Bodrum'a/ Kuşadası'na otobüs be zaman kalkıyor? (b) Saat dokuzu on geçe. Saat dokuz buçukta. Saat on da. Saat onu kırk geçe (or Saat onbire yirmi kala). (c) Efes'e otobüs ne zaman varacak? İzmir'e otobüs ne zaman varacak? Bodrum'a otobüs ne zaman varacak? Kuşadası'na otobüs ne zaman varacak?
3.6 You: Kuşadası'na gitmek istiyorum. You: Bu sabah. You: İki kişi için. You: Bir bilet ne kadar? You: Lütfen iki gidiş bileti You: İşte 15 000 lira, teşekkürler.

4.1 You: Ben biraz İngiliz sterlin banknotu değiştirmek istiyorum. You: Yüz sterlin. Bugün döviz kuru nedir? You: Teşekkürler.
4.2 Benim pasaportum. Benim seyehat çeklerim. Benim İstanbul'a tren biletim. Benim Kredi kartım. Benim Türk paralarım.
4.3 You: İyi günler, efendim. İngiltere'ye iki kartpostal pulu, lütfen. You: Teşekkürler. Amerika'ya dört

mektup pulu lütfen.
You: Evet, tamam. Hepsi ne kadar tutar?
You: İşte paranız. Affedersiniz,
Londra'ya telefon edebilir miyim?
You: Çok teşekkürler, hoşça kalınız.
4.4 1 Posta pulu satın almalıyım. 2
Avusturalya'ya bir paket
göndermeliyim. 3 Bankaya gitmeliyim.
4.Biraz seyehat çekleri bozdurmalıyım.
5 Otobüs terminaline gitmeliyim. 6
İzmir'e bir bilet satın almalıyım.
5.1 Biz küçük bir araba istiyoruz. 2 Üç
gün için kaç lira? 3 Depozite ödemeli
miyim? 4 Biz, Peugeot'u istiyoruz. Lütfen
anahtarı veriniz. 5 Arabayı Antalya'da
bırakabilir miyiz? (teslim
edebilirmiyiz?)
5.2 Lütfen 30 litrelik süper benzin
veriniz. 2 Lütfen lastiklerin havasına bir
bakınız. 3 Tamir yapıyor musunuz (or
onarabilir misiniz?) 4 Bir kayış satın
almak istiyorum. 5 Lütfen fatura veriniz.
5.3 Trafik polisi, garaj/oto tamircisi,
. . . .
5.4 1 Affedersiniz, garaj nerededir? 2
Arabamız bozuldu. 3 Benzinimiz
tükendi. 4 Bir bakar mısınız?
5.5 You: İshal için bir şeyiniz var mı?
You: Peki, tamam. Günde kaç tane
almalıyım?
You: Teşekkürler. Kaç lira?
5.6 Kate: Güneşte yandım. David:
Midem ağrıyor. Peter: Ayak – bileğim
burkuldu. Maggie: Kolumu yaktım. You:
Ben de, plajda düştüm ve dizimi
incittim.
5.7 2 Anahtarımı kaybettim. 4 Fotoğraf
makinemi kaybettim. 1 Pasaportumu
kaybettim. 3 El çantamı kaybettim. 5
Biletimi kaybettim.

6.1 1 Ben tenis oynamasını severim. 2
Ben futbol seyretmesini severim. 3 Ben
yelkenciliği severim. 6 Ben ata binmeyi
severim. 4 Ben kayak yapmayı severim.
5 Ben golf oynamasını severim. 7 Ben
yüzmeyi severim. 8 Ben yürümeyi
severim.
6.2 Biz tenis oynamak istiyoruz. Boş bir
tenis sahası var mı?
Bu sabah, saat onbir gibi olabilir.
Tamam, Bir kaç tenis topu kiralamak
istiyorum.
6.3 1 Stadyom nerede dir?

2 Yüzme havuzu nerede dir? 3 Su
kayağı yarışması nerededir? 4
Basketbol turnuvası nerededir?
6.4 Fasl-ı Konak

1 Yemek ve Türk Sanat Müzik
  Progamı.
2 Türk sanat ve Hafif Müziği
3 Her hafta pazartesi ve perşembe
  geceleri.
4 Bir kişi için otuz beş bin lira (35,000
  T.L.).

İstanbul Geceleri
1 Istanbul'da yemekli bir Türk Müzik
  Gecesi
2 Türk sanat, halk ve hafif müzikleri.
3 Herakşam, saat 20.30 da.
4 Yemekli kırk bin lira (40,000 T.L.)

7.1 Mark: Ben bir mimarım. Susan:
Ben bir muhasebeciyim. Anna: Ben bir
taksi şoförüyüm. Charles: Ben bir iş
adamıyım. Bernard: Ben bir çöpcüyün. .
Helen: Ben bir artistim. Mesleğiniz
nedir?
7.2 1 İstanbul'da hava nasıl? 2 İzmir'de
yağmur yağıyor mu? 3 Dağlar da kar
yağıyor mu? 4 Güney Kıyılaı rüzgarlı mı?
7.3 1 Name 2 Surname 3 Date of birth
4 Place of birth 5 Marital Status
6 Occupation 7 Work place 8 Hobbies
9 Preferred sports 10 Preferred music
11 Preferred branches of art 12
Preferred colours 13 Preferred
countries
7.4 A 1 Ben, klasik müziği severim. 2
Ben, keman ve piyano çalarım. 3 Ben,
haftada bir defa konsere giderim. 4
Ben, pazartesi akşamları bir müzik
kulübüne giderim. B 1 Ben, bir
sanatkarım. 2 Resim çizerim ve sulu
boya yaparım. 3 Ben, perşembe
sabahları çömlekçilik kursuna giderim.
4 Ben, bütün sergilere giderim.

VOCABULARY

Numbers

1	bir	19	ondokuz	70	yetmiş		
2	iki	20	yirmi	80	seksen		
3	üç	21	yirmibir	90	doksan		
4	dört	22	yirmiiki	100	yüz		
5	beş	23	yirmiüç	200	ikiyüz		
6	altı	24	yirmidört	900	dokuzyüz		
7	yedi	25	yirmibeş	1000	bin		
8	sekiz	26	yirmialtı	8000	sekizbin		
9	dokuz	27	yirmiyedi				
10	on	28	yirmisekiz				
11	onbir	29	yirmidokuz	first	birinci		
12	oniki	30	otuz	second	ikinci		
13	onüç	31	otuzbir	third	üçüncü		
14	ondört	32	otuziki	fourth	dördüncü		
15	onbeş		etc	fifth	beşinci		
16	onaltı	40	kırk		etc		
17	onyedi	50	elli	ninth	dokuzuncu		
18	onsekiz	60	altmış	tenth	onuncu		

Months

January	Ocak	July	Temmuz
February	Şubat	August	Ağustos
March	Mart	September	Eylül
April	Nisan	October	Ekim
May	Mayıs	November	Kasım
June	Haziran	December	Aralık

Seasons

Spring	İlkbahar
Summer	Yaz
Autumn	Sonbahar
Winter	Kış

Clothes

belt	kayış	overall	iş elbisesi
blouse	gömlek	pyjamas	pijama
bra	sütyen	raincoat	yağmurluk
coat	palto-manto	scarf	atkı
dress	elbise	shirt	gömlek
gloves	eldiven	skirt	etek
handbag	el çantası	socks	çoraplar
hat	şapka	stockings	kadın çorabı
jacket	ceket	suit	takım elbise
jeans	blujin	nightdress	gecelik
trousers	pantalon	underpants	kilot

Colours

black	siyah, kara	pink	pembe	light	açık
blue	mavi	red	kırmızı	dark blue	koyu mavi
brown	kahverengi	white	beyaz	light grey	açık gri
green	yeşil	yellow	sarı		
grey	gri	dark	koyu		

VOCABULARY

Materials

cotton	**pamuk**	silk	**ipek**	velvet	**kadife**
leather	**deri**	silken	**ipekli**	wool	**yün**
nylon	**naylon**	suede	**süed**	woollen	**yünlü**

At the chemists

antiseptic	**antiseptik**	painkiller	**ağrı kesici**
bandage	**sargı bezi**	plaster	**band**
cotton wool	**pamuk**	prescription	**reçete**
cough syrup	**öksürük şurubu**	sleeping pills	**uyku hapı**
duty chemist	**nöbetci eczane**	thermometer	**termometre**
medicine	**ilaç**	throat pills	**boğaz yumuşatıcı**
ointment	**merhem**		

Toiletries

baby food	**bebek maması**	razor	**jilet**
brush	**fırça**	safety pins	**çengelli iğne**
comb	**tarak**	shampoo	**şampuvan**
cream	**krem**	soap	**sabun**
deodorant	**deodorant**	suntan lotion	**güneş yağı**
electric razor	**elektrikli traş makinesi**	tissues	**kağıt mendil**
		toothpaste	**diş macunu**
perfume	**parfüm**	toothbrush	**diş fırçası**

Food

Menu (general words)

barbecued	**meşe kömürde ızgara**	fish dishes	**balık yemekleri**
		fried	**kızartma**
boiled	**haşlama**	fruits	**meyvalar**
casseroled	**güveçte**	grilled	**izgarada**
desserts	**tatlılar**	soups	**çorbalar**
dishes with meat	**etli yemekler**	starters	**mezeler**
dishes with olive oil	**zeytinyağlı yemekleri**	vegetables	**sebzeler**

Starters

aubergine salad	**patlıcan salatası**	fried mussels	**midye tava**
		mixed salad	**karışık salata**
carrot salad	**havuç salatası**	pinto bean dish	**barbunya pilaki**
chicken circassian	**çerkez tavuğu**		
cucumber in yoghurt	**cacık**	shepherds salad	**çoban salatası**
dry red beans dish	**pilaki**	stuffed mussels	**midye dolması**
fried aubergines	**patlıcan kızartması**		
courgettes	**kabak ...**		
pepper	**biber ...**		

VOCABULARY

Soups

flour soup	**un çorbası**	tripe soup	**işkembe çorbası**
red lentils soup	**kırmızı mercimek çorbası**	vegetable soup	**sebze çorbası**
		wedding soup	**düğün çorbası**
semolina soup	**irmik çorbası**	yoghurt soup	**yoğurtlu çorba**

Some fish dishes

fillets of sole	**dil filetosu**
grey mullet with vegetables	**kefal pilakisi**
mackerel in sauce	**Salçalı uskumru**
salt cured tuna	**lakerda**
sea bass in white wine	**Beyaz şarap soslu levrek**
skewered shrimp	**karides şiş**
steamed anchovies	**hamsi buğulama**
swordfish	**kılıç**
turbot	**kalkan**

Some meat dishes

forest kebab	**orman kebabı**	meat balls, dry	**kuru köfte**
gardener's kebab	**bahçevan kebabı**	meat balls, in tomato	**İzmir köftesi**
		shish kebab	**şiş kebabı**
hunters kebab	**avcı kebabı**	sultan's delight	**hünkar beğendi**
kebab casserole	**güveç kebabı**	woman's casserole	**hanım güveci**
kebab with yoghurt	**yoğurtlu kebap**		
meat balls, chicken	**tavuk köftesi**		

Poultry

chicken with rice	**pirinçli piliç**
cream chicken	**kremalı piliç**
duck with mushrooms	**mantarlı ördek**
roasted chicken	**fırında piliç kızartması**

Vegetable dishes

broad beans in oil	**zeytin yağlı bakla**
fresh green beans dish	**taze fasulye**
fried potatoes	**patates kızartması**
green peas dish	**taze bezelye**
leek with rice	**zeytinyağlı pırasa**
mixed vegetable dish	**türlü**
mousakka	**patlıcan musaka**
potato dish	**etli patates**
stuffed vegetables	**dolma**
aubergine	**patlıcan dolması**
courgettes	**kabak dolması**
peppers	**biber dolması**
tomatoes	**domates dolması**
vine leaves	**yaprak dolması**

(Hot dolmas are with meat, cold dolmas are starters)

VOCABULARY

Pastries

Cigarette pastry with cheese	**peynirli sigara böreği**
pastry with meat	**kıymalı börek**
with cheese	**peynirli börek**
with spinach	**ıspanaklı börek**
pizza with cheese	**peynirli pide**
with meat	**kıymalı pide**
with egg	**yumurtalı pide**
with Turkish salami	**sucuklu pide**
water pastry with cheese	**peynirli su böreği**
with meat	**kıymalı su böreği**

Desserts

baklava	**baklava**		ladies naval	**hanım göbeği**
beauty's lips	**dilber dudağı**		milk pudding	**muhallebi**
cake in syrup	**revani**		semolina helva	**irmik helvası**
chicken breasts	**tavuk göğsü**		vanilla pudding	**keşkül**
kadaif	**kadayıf**			

Fruit

apples	**elma**		peaches	**şeftali**
apricots	**kayısı**		pears	**armut**
banana	**muz**		plum	**erik**
cherry	**vişne**		pomegranate	**nar**
figs	**incir**		quince	**ayva**
grapes	**üzüm**		strawberry	**çilek**
lemon	**limon**		sweet melons	**kavun**
mulberries	**dut**		water melons	**karpuz**
orange	**portakal**			

Groceries

biscuits	**biskuvit**		margarine	**sanayağı**
bread	**ekmek**		milk	**süt**
cheese	**peynir**		oil	**likit yağ**
coffee	**kahve**		pasta	**makarna**
eggs	**yumurta**		rice	**pirinç**
flour	**un**		sugar	**şeker**
jam	**reçel**		tea	**çay**

Parts of the body

ankle	**ayak bileği**	finger	**parmak**		lip	**dudak**
arm	**kol**	foot	**ayak**		mouth	**ağız**
back	**sırt**	hair	**saç**		neck	**boyun**
chest	**göğüs**	hand	**el**		shoulder	**omuz**
ear	**kulak**	head	**baş**		skin	**deri**
elbow	**dirsek**	heart	**kalp**		stomach	**karın, mide**
eye	**göz**	hip	**kalça**		throat	**boğaz**
eyes	**gözler**	knee	**diz**		tooth	**diş**
face	**yüz**	leg	**bacak**			

83

VOCABULARY

Sports

basketball	**basketbol**	jogging	**koşma**
billiards	**bilardo**	sailing	**yelkencilik**
chess	**santranç**	scuba-diving	**dalgıçlık**
climbing	**tırmanış**	shooting	**atıcılık**
fishing	**balık avlama**	skiing	**kayakçılık**
flying	**uçuş**	swimming	**yüzme**
football	**futbol**	tennis	**tenis**
golf	**golf**	volleyball	**voleybol**
horse racing	**binicilik, atcılık**		

Parts of the car

battery	**akü**	indicator	**sinyal lambası**
brakes	**frenler**	petrol tank	**benzin tankı**
clutch	**debriyaj**	plugs	**bujiler**
distributor	**distribütör**	radiator	**radyatör**
engine	**motor**	steering wheel	**direksiyon**
exhaust	**egzos**	tyres	**araba lastikleri**
fan-belt	**motor kayışı**	wheels	**tekerlekler**
gears	**vitesler**	windscreen	**araba ön camı**
headlights	**uzun fenerler/farlar**	wipers	**cam silecekleri**
ignition	**manş anahtarı**	bulbs	**ampüller**

Professions

accountant	**muhasebeci**
architect	**mimar**
bank clerk	**banka memuru**
banker	**bankacı, banker**
builder	**inşaatcı**
businessman	**iş adamı**
businesswoman	**iş hanımı**
chef	**ahçı başı, şef**
chemist	**eczacı, kimyager**
civil servant	**devlet memuru**
company director	**firma direktörü**
computer programmer	**kompüter programlayıcısı**
computer operator	**kompüter operatörü**
dentist	**dişçi, diş doktoru**
doctor	**hekim, tabib, doktor**
engineer	**mühendis**
(civil)	**inşaat mühendisi**
(chemical)	**kimya mühendisi**
(electronic)	**elektronik mühendisi**
estate agent	**emlakçı**
hairdresser	**kadın berberi**
housewife	**ev hanımı**
interpreter	**tercüman**
journalist	**gazeteci**
mechanic	**araba tamircisi, ustası**
nurse	**hemşire, hasta bakıcı**

VOCABULARY

policeman		polis
salesman		satış uzmanı
secretary		sekreter
solicitor		avukat, noter
student		öğrenci
teacher		öğretmen

Work places

bank	banka	garage	garaj
clinic	kilinik	hospital	hastahane
college	kolej	laboratory	laboratuvar
factory	fabrika	office	ofis
firm	firma	shop	dükkan

---

acaba I wonder if
acele hurry, urgent, hurried action, at once
acı pain, ache, hot (pepper etc.)
acil Hastanesi emergency hospital
aç hungry
açık open
ad name
adet (or tane) a single item
adres address
aferin (or **aferim**) bravo, well done
affetmek to excuse (person)
affedersiniz I beg your pardon; excuse me
afiyet health
afiyetle with a good appetite
afiyet olsun bon appetit
ağrımak to ache, hurt, to suffer pain
ağrı kesici pain killer
ağrıyan aching, hurting
aile family
Akdeniz the Mediterranean
akşam evening
alerji allergy
alet tool, implement
alıcı customer, receiver
alış-veriş shopping

almak to take
alınmak to be taken
ambülans ambulance
ana (or anne) mother
anahtar key
anlamak to understand, to comprehend
araba car, automobile
aramak to search, to look for
arasıra now and then, from time to time, occasionally
arka back, back side, rear
arkadaş friend, fellow
artist actor, actress,
arzu wish, want, request
arzu etmek to wish for, to long for, to desire
astım (astımlı) asthma (asthma sufferer)
aşağı down, downwards
aşağıda below, downstairs
at horse
atcılık horse riding, horses
Avrupa Europe
ay month, moon
ayırtmak to have reserved
ayrılmak to part, to leave
az few, not much, little

baba father
bagaj luggage
bahçe garden, park
bakmak to look (at), to pay attention to
balık fish
balkon balcony
balkonlu with balcony
bana to me
banka bank
banka kartı bank card
banknot banknote
banyo bath, bathroom
banyolu with bath
bar bar
bardak cup, mug, glass
basketbol basketball
baş head, start, beginning
başka other, another, different
başlamak to begin, to start
bavul suitcase
bazen sometimes
belediye otobüsü public bus
belki perhaps, maybe
ben I
benim mine
benzin petrol
benzinci filling station
beyan declaration
beyaz peynir white curd cheese

VOCABULARY

bıçak knife
biber pepper
bilet ticket
bilmek to know
bira beer
biraz a little, some
birinci the first
birkaç a few, some
bisiklet bicycle
bizce according to us, in our opinion
bizim our, ours
boğaz olmak to have a sore throat
boş empty, vacant, free
bozdurmak to have (money) changed
bozuk broken, out of order
bozuk para small change, coins
bozulmak to become out of order, to break down
bölge region, district
böyle like this
bu this
bunlar these
buçuk and a half
bugün today
bulanmak (miğde) to be upset (stomach)
bulut cloud
bulutlu cloudy
bura this place, here
burada in this place, here
burkmak or **Burkulmak** to sprain (a joint), to twist
burkulma twisting, twist
buyurun or **buyurunuz** please come in; help yourself, here it is, take it, welcome
büfe buffet
büro office
bütün whole, entire, total, complete
büyük great, large, big, elder
cadde main road in a city

cami mosque
can soul, life
ceket jacket
cerrah surgeon
cümbüş kind of mandolin with metal body
çabucak quickly
çabuk quick, fast, quickly
çağırmak to call, to invite
çalgı (or **çalgı aleti**) musical instrument
çalmak to play a musical instrument
çalınmak to be stolen
çalışmak to work, to study, to try
çanta bag, case
çarşı shopping market
çatal fork
çay tea
çek cheque
çek kartı cheque card
çektirmek to have (it) taken
çeşit kind, sort, variety
çevirmek to turn, to change (into), to dial (a telephone)
çeyrek a quarter
çıkış exit,
çıkmak to exit
çift couple, pair, double
çoban shepherd
çocuk child, infant
çocuk bahçesi children's playground
çok much, a lot
çömlek earthenware pot
çömlekcilik pottery

da (de, ta, te) too, also
dan beri (den beri etc) since
dağ mountain
dağcı mountaineer
dağcılık mountaineering
daha more, further
dahil including
dakika minute
dal branch

dans dance
dans etmek to dance
dansöz dancer (f)
darbuka small drum
davet invitation
davul large drum
defa (or kere) time, turn, again
değerli valuable, worth
değil not
değişik different
değiştirmek to exchange (for), to change
deniz sea
depozite deposit, security
derhal at once, immediately
ders lesson
dış outside, exterior
dışında outside of
dışarı outdoors
dışarıda outside
diğer the other, next
dikkat be careful, look out!
dilim slice, strip
dişçi (or **diş doktoru**) dentist
diyabetik diabetes
doğan falcon, hawk
doğru right, correct, straight, direct
doğum birth
doğum evi or **hastahanesi** maternity hospital
doğum kontrol hapı (birth control) pill
doğum tarihi birth date
doğum yeri place of birth
doktor doctor
doldurmak to fill in
dolmuş shared taxi
dolmuşcu dolmuş driver
dolu full, hail stones
dosdoğru straight ahead, straight on
dönmek to turn round, to go round
dörtyol crossroads
döviz foreign exchange
döviz kuru foreign exchange rates
durak stop (bus, dolmuş)

duş shower
duşlu with shower
düğme button, switch
dükkan shop
dün yesterday
düşmek to fall
düşünmek to think

eczacı chemist
eczane chemist's, drugstore
eğlence entertainment
ehliyet driving licence
ekip team, company
ekmek bread
elde dokunmuş handwoven
elçilik embassy
elektronik electronic
elektrik electrical
elma apple
el sanatı handicrafts
en most
enformasyon (or informasyon) information
erkek man, male
erken (or erkenden) early
ertesi the next, the following (day, week etc.)
eski old
eskitmek to wear out, to use up
eş partner, husband or wife
eşya things, objects, furniture
etyemez vegetarian
ev house
ev hanımı housewife
evet yes
evvel before, earlier
evvelki gün the day before

fabrika firm, company, manufacturing company
fakat but
fatura receipt, bill
fazla excess, more
feribot ferry boat
fırtına storm, gale

fiş coupon, form
fiyat price
folklör folk
fotoğraf photography, photograph
fotoğraf makinesi camera

gar railway station
garson waiter
gaz gas, (accelerator in car)
gazete newspaper
gece night
gecelik for a night
geç late, delayed
geçen hafta last week
geçmek to pass
geçmiş olsun get well soon
gelmek to come (from, to), to arrive
genel general
genellikle (or genel olarak) in general
gerçek real, true, genuine
gerçekten in fact, actually, really
gerekmek to be necessary, needed, required
geri back, backward, behind
getirmek to fetch, to bring
gibi like
gidiş departure, going
gidiş–geliş or gidiş-dönüş return (ticket)
gişe memuru ticket officer
gitar guitar
gitmek to go, to leave, to depart
golf golf
göndermek to send, to dispatch
gönderen sender
görmek to see
göre (-(e) göre) according to, in respect of
görülmek to be seen

görüş seeing, opinion, observation
görüşmek to meet, to see each other
götürmek to take away, to carry off
gül rose
güle güle goodbye
gümrük custom, duty, tariff
gün day
güneş – güneşli sun, sunny
güneş yanığı sunburn
günlük (or gün başına) per day, daily
gürültü noise
güzel beautiful, pretty, nice

hafif light
hafif müzik Turkish pop music
hafta week
hakiki genuine, true, real
halk folk, people, nation
halk müziği folk music
hamile pregnant
hangi which
hap pill, medicine, tablet
harabe ruins
hareket departure
hareket etmek to start, to set out on, to move
harita map
hasta sick, ill, unwell, patient
hasta bakıcı nurse
hastahane hospital
hata mistake, error, fault
hava air, atmosphere, weather
hava basmak. to put air into something
hava durumu weather situation
hava raporu weather, report
hava alanı airport
havlu towel
havuz pool, pond
hayat live, living

VOCABULARY

haydi (or hadi!) come on
hayır no
hazımsızlık indigestion
hazır ready, prepared
hazır olmak to be ready
hediye gift, present
hemen at once, right now
hemen hemen almost, very nearly
hemşire nurse
henüz only now, yet, still
hepsi all of it
hepsi bu kadar that is all!
her every, each
hesap bill, account
hissetmek to feel
hobi hobby
hoş pleasant, agreeable
hoş bulduk I am pleased to see you, thank you (in response to **hoş geldiniz**.)
hoş geldiniz welcome
hoşa gitmek or **hoşuna gitmek** to please, to be agreeable to
hoşlanmak to like, to be pleased with, to enjoy

içmek to drink, to smoke
içecek drink, beverage, drinkable
içeri inside
içeride inside, within
içerik contents
için for, in order to
içinde within, in
içki alcoholic drink
iğne needle, pin, injection
iğne yapmak to give an injection
ilaç medicine, drug
ile with
ileri further on, forward, front
ilginç interesting
ılık tepid, lukewarm
ilk yardım first aid
imdat Help!
imek to be
imza signature
imzalamak to sign

incelemek to examine carefully
incinmek to be sprained, to be injured
incitmek to hurt, to injure, to sprain
insan man, human being
inşallah God willing, if God wills, I hope so
ipek silk, silken
iplik thread, yarn, fibre
ishal diarrhoea
ishal olmak to have diarrhoea
isim name, title
istasyon station, railway station, stop
istemek to want, to require, to need
iş work, business, occupation
iş adamı businessman
ışık light
iş yeri work place
işsiz unemployed
işte here, thus, oh well, like that
itfaiye fire brigade
iyi good, well, in good health
izin permission, leave, permit

jiklet chewing gum

kabul etmek to accept, to agree, to approve
kaç how many? how much?
kaça what is the price?
kadar as much as, as many as, as . . . as
kağıt paper
kahvaltı breakfast
kahve coffee
kahvehane coffee shop, café
kalmak to remain, to stay, to stop
kalabalık crowded
kale castle, fortress
kalkmak to set out on a journey, to start
kambiyo foreign exchange

kambiyo memuru bank clerk for foreign transactions
kamyon lorry, truck
kanun a zither-like musical string instrument
kapalı shut, closed, overcast
kar snow
karlı snowy
kar yağmak to snow
karakol police station
karavan caravan
karışık mixed, complex
karşı opposite, opposite side or direction
karşılaşmak to meet one another
karşılık return, equivalent
kartpostal postcard
kaset çalar tape player, cassette player
kaşık spoon
kat floor, stage
katılmak to join in, to participate
katip clerk
kayak (kayak yapmak) ski (to ski)
kaybetmek to lose
kaybolmak to be lost
kayık boat, rowing boat
kayıp loss
kayıp eşya ofisi lost property office
kayış belt, strap
kaza accident, mishap
keman violin
kendi oneself
kendim myself
kırmak to break, to injure
kırık broken
kırılmak to be broken
kısa short
kış winter
kışın in winter
kıyı short, coast, edge
kız girl, daughter
kilim flat, woven rug
kilo kilogram
kilosu per kilogram

VOCABULARY

kilo vermek or **kilo kaybetmek** or **kilo atmak** to lose weight
kilometre kilometre
kilometre başına per kilometre
kiralamak to rent, to hire
kiralık for rent, for hire
kirli dirty, unclean
kişi person, individual
kişilik for (so many) persons
klasik classical
klasik müzik classical music
kod code
kolay easy
kolayca/kolaylıkla easily
kolej a kind of grammar school
komple complete
vilayet konağı town hall
konser concert
kontrol checking
kontrol etmek to check
konuksever hospitable
konuşma conversation, dialogue
konuşmak to talk, to chat, to speak
kopuk broken apart, torn away
korkmak to be afraid, to fear
koşmak to run
köpek dog
köşe corner
köşebaşı street corner, the corner
köy village
köylü villager
kredi credit
kredi kartı credit card
kullanmak to use
kullanılmak to be used
kulüp club
kurs course (of lessons etc.)
kuru dry, dried
kutu small box or case
küçük small, little, young

kültablası ashtray
kültür culture
lastik tyre, rubber
lazım necessary
lazım olmak to be necessary
leziz delicious, tasty
liman harbour, seaport
liste list, menu
lokanta restaurant
lütfen please

macera adventure
maden suyu mineral water
mağaza large store, shop
masa table
medeni durum marital status
mektup letter
memnun pleased, happy
memnun olmak to be pleased, to be happy
memur official, civil servant, officer
merak etmek to be anxious about someone or something
merak etmeyiniz please, don't worry
merdiven steps, stairs
merkez centre
meslek occupation, profession, career
metre metre
mevsim season
meyva fruit
meyva suyu fruit juice
milliyet nationality
misafir guest, visitor
modern modern
motel motel
motifli patterned
motorsiklet motorcycle
müdür director, manager
müze museum

nakit para cash, ready money
nasıl how
nasılsınız? how are you?

ne what, how (with adjectives), which
neden why
nefes breath, breathing
nefes almak to breathe, to take a breath
nefis excellent, exquisite
ne kadar how much
ne kadar süre (or zaman) how long (time)
nemli moist, damp
nere where
nerede (in, at, on) where
nereden/nereli from where
nerelisiniz? where are you from?
nereye where to
ne zaman when
nezle a cold
nezle olmak to catch a cold
niçin why? what for?
normal normal
nöbetçi eczane chemist on duty (rota basis)
numara number
numaralı numbered

o that, he, she, it
oda room
ofis office
oğul son
okumak to read
okul school
okunmak to be read
olmak to be, to happen, to occur, to become
onarmak to repair
onlar those, they
onların their, theirs
onun his, her, hers, its, of him, her
ora that place, there
orada there
oradan from there
oraya to there
otel hotel
oto car
otobüs bus
otopark car park
otobüs terminali bus station, coach terminal

oynamak to play, to play a game/a sport
oyun game, play, dance
o zaman then

ödemek to pay
öğlende, öğleyin at noon
öğleden sonra in the afternoon
öğrenmek to learn
öğretmen teacher
ön front
önde in the front
önden from the front
öne to the front
önünde in front of
önce (-den önce) before, first, at first
önemli important
örnek example, specimen, sample
özel personal, private, special
özellikle specially, particularly
özür dilemek to ask pardon, to beg to be excused

pahalı expensive
paket parcel, package
palto overcoat
pamuk cotton
pamuk ipliği cotton thread, çotton yarn
pansiyon boarding house, room
para money
para çekmek to withdraw (money from bank)
para yatırmak to deposit, to invest money in bank
parça small, piece
park park, garden, park
park etmek (or yapmak) to part (a car etc.)
pasaport passport
patlak burst, flat (tyre)
pazar Sunday, market
peçete table napkin
pek very, much
pekala, peki, pekiyi very well, ok., very good, all right
pek çok very much

pencere window
penisilin penicillin
piyano piano
plaj beach
poliklinik polyclinic, clinic for out-patients
polis police
pompa pump
porsiyon portion
posta mail, post, postal service
postacı postman
posta pulu postage stamp
posta memuru post office clerk
posta kutusu post box
postahane post office
program programme
pul stamp
puslu hazy, misty

radyo radio
raket racket
reçete prescription
renk colour
renkli coloured
resepsiyon reception
resepsiyoncu receptionist
resim picture, drawing
resim çizmek to draw, to sketch
restoran restaurant
röntgen filmi X-ray
rüzgar wind, breeze
rüzgarlı windy
rüzgar esmek to blow a wind

saat hour, time
saat kaç? what time is it?
saat kaçta? At what time? When?
sabah morning
sabahleyin in the morning
sağ right
sağa to the right
sağda on the right side
sağdan from the right side
saha court, field, ground
(tenis sahası, tennis court
basketbol sahası) basketball ground

saman nezlesi hay fever
sanat art, craft
sanatçı (sanatkar) artisan, craftsman, artist
sanat müziği Turkish classical music
sanmak to suppose, to think
sandalye chair
sapmak to deviate, to turn
sarma wound, wrapped
satıcı seller
satın almak to buy, to purchase
satış selling
saz Turkish lute
semaver samovar
sen you (singular)
sende on you
senden from you
seni your, yours
seninle with you
seramik ceramic
sergi exhibition, show
servis service
sevilmek to be loved, liked
sevmek to love, to like
seyehat journey, travel
seyehat çeki traveller's cheque
seyretmek to watch
sıcak hot
sıfır zero
sigorta insurance
sinema cinema
sırt back
sis fog, mist
sisli foggy, misty
siyah black, dark coloured
siz you (plural, polite)
sizce according to you
size to you
sizde at you
siz den from you
sizin your, yours
sizinle with you
sürücü driver
soğuk cold
sokak road, street
sol left
sola to the left side

solda on the left side
soldan from the left side
son end, last
sonunda finally, in the end
sonra later, afterwards
soyadı surname
soyunmak to undress (one self)
soyunma odası changing room
söylemek to say, to speak
spor sport
stadyom stadium
su water
su kayağı waterskiing
sulu boya watercolour (paint)
sunmak to present, to offer
sunulmak to be performed, presented
süper superb, extra better
sürmek to drive (a car), to take (time)
susmak to be silent, to be quiet
susamak to be thirsty, to thirst
susuz waterless, thirsty, dry
şahsi personal, private
şans luck
şanslı olmak to be lucky
şarap wine
şarkı song
şehir city
şeker sugar
şey thing
bir şey değil you're welcome, don't mention it
şimdi now
şirket company
şiş spit, skewer
şişe bottle, flask
şişmek to swell, to inflate
şöyle like that
şu that
şunlar those
şura that place

şurada in that place
şöför driver
taahhütlü registered (letter etc.)
tabak plate, dish
taksi taxi
tam complete, exact, entire, whole
tamam complete, okay, correct, very well
tamir etmek (or yapmak) to repair, to mend
tane a single individual item
taraf side
tarih history
tanışmak to get acquainted with
tanıştırmak to introduce to one another
tartmak to weigh
tatil holiday
tavsiye etmek to recommend
taze fresh, new
tehlike danger, risk
tek a single item
tekerlek wheel, (tyre)
telefon telephone
telefonlu with a telephone
telefon etmek to phone
telefon kulübesi telephone kiosk
televizyon television
telgraf telegraph
temiz clean, pure
tenis tennis
tenis topu tennis ball
teras terrace
tercih etmek to prefer
tereyağı butter
terminal terminal
tesbih worry beads
teslim etmek to deliver, to hand over
teşekkür thank
teşekkür etmek to thank
top ball
trafik traffic
trafik hastahanesi traffic accident hospital

trafik polisi traffic policeman
tren train
turist tourist
turist rehberi tourist guide
turizm tourism
tutmak to total up, to come to . . .
tuvalet lavatory, toilet
tuz salt
tükenmek to be exhausted, to run out
tünaydın good evening
ucuz cheap
uçak airplane
uçuş flight, flying
ulak courier
özel ulak special courier
uluslararası international
usta master (of a trade or craft)
uyumak to sleep, to go to sleep
uzak far away
uzun long, tall
uzun araç (TIR-kamyonu) long lorry (HGV)

ücret price
ülke country
üzere on, upon, on the subject of
üzülmek to be sorry
üzüm grape

vapur steamer, passenger boat
var to exist, to have
varmak to arrive at, to reach
vazo vase
ve and, also, too
vermek to give, to deliver
veya or
vezne cashier's office, cash desk
vites gears (automobile)
vites kutusu gearbox (automobile)
voleybol volley-ball

yağ oil, fat, butter
yağmak to rain
yağlı oily, fatty, in oil
yağlı boya oil paint

yağmur (yağmurlu) rain (rainy)

yağmur yağmak to rain

yağ pompası oil pump

yakmak to burn, to scorch

yakın near, nearby

yaklaşık approximately, about

yalnız alone, only

yan side

yangın fire

yangın söndürücü fire extinguisher

yanlış error, mistake, wrong

yanlışlık error, mistake, blunder

yapmak to do, to make

yaprak leaf

yaralı wounded, hurt

yardım help

yardım etmek to help

yarım half

yarın tomorrow

yasak prohibited, forbidden

yaşamak to live, to reside

yaşantı manner of living, life

yatak bed

yataklı furnished with a bed

yavaş slow, gentle

yavaşça slowly, gently

yaya pedestrian, passer-by

yayla high plateau

yaz summer

yazın in the summer

yazlık for summer use

yazmak to write

yedek parça spare part

yelken sailing boat

yelkencilik sailing

yemek food, meal

yemek yemek to eat

yeni new

yer place

yerine in place of, instead of

yetki authority

yetkili qualified, responsible

yıl year

yok not to exist, not to have

yoksa if not, otherwise, or else

yol road

yolculuk travel, journey

yorucu tiring

yöntem method, way

yörük Turcoman

yukarı up, above, upwards

yün wool, woollen

yün iplik wool, yarn

yürümek to walk

yürüme walking

yürüyerek on foot, by walking

yüzmek to swim

yüzme havuzu swimming pool

yüzme simidi rubber ring

zengin rich

zeytin olive

ziyaret visit

iş ziyareti business visit

zor difficult